Apex Unhinged

by Zeero Xiron

To Holly,

wherever you might be.

Apex Unhinged

Bring On The Death Trump

Insanity is a gift bestowed upon the unprepared. Curse and blessing at once, there is luminous truth behind the cracked mirror. I assure you, people receive The Vision Of The Throne Of God. It does not arrive in the package assumed, yet onward it comes – bulldozes & rearranges...

This is a story about how I went insane, came back, lost it again, regenerated & collapsed only to crawl out from the ruins of The Tower to face The Star. How I was driven to lunacy by stark reality and forced to exchange one madness for another.

How I was reborn to Magick and went homeless for years before Covid broke out, and subsequently how this pandemic sealed my destiny to 3 more years of homelessness in crumbled Portland. How I found my New Voice but soon went totally schizophrenic, entrapping me in the depths of the psych ward. Most importantly, it is how I learned my mind could randomly be taken to new extreme & traumatic places on the drop of a dime.

My name is Zeero Xiron. It wasn't always my name, but it sure is now. Magick does that to you – you project a character and end up that character by default. That's kind of the point to begin with, even though you don't recognize it at first. It's all about the Crooked Path. You set out on the journey and it takes you wherever it may. If it was easy, or linear, there would be no true growth. Whatever you set out to become you end up something else.

I am a Magickal Supervillain + aspiring Heretic Ipsissimus practicing Cosmic Witchcraft & High Magick upon a framework of Heretic Druidry, Qabalah, Ninjutsu, Hermetic & Pythagorean Philosophy. I promote Spiritual & Psychological Alchemy, Ritual Magick, Tarot & more.

I'm a non-Abrahamic Monotheist who observes Architect & Creation. Regardless, I am Pagan in that I worship nature in a universal sense + accept many Deities & Daemons as valid masks & aspects of The Creation. Gods & Goddesses are projections of our own being or Totems entailing forces of nature, not literal beings. I oppose Buddha, Christ & Abrahamic God visions. ALL is ALL. Welcome to the Wonder-filled World of the Dr. Zeero Xiron Free Magick Secrets Show.

Anyway, I used to write books as some Other Guy. His books are horror shows – nightmare memoirs that are not fun to write. Truth is I just want to hammer this one out and be free of it. This manuscript oozes out of me like a 5 foot pimple.

I have been misunderstood at nearly every level my entire life and I equally misunderstood the world. There was not one adult who ever sat me down and explained how life worked in any tangible sense, no significant advice on how to proceed or what I would actually have to do to survive. Everything was shielded as long as it could be, or obfuscated, or handed to me in "wise" sayings and stereotype explanations.

The world of the homeless was hidden from me. Lower middle class I was, son of a rotten soil and ignorant environment full of bigotry, racism & homophobia. Compared with the community standards of Portland, the world that reared me was 100 years behind.

All the key players in my life died long ago or are simply pictures on social media. I'm what's left – good ol' Zeero Xiron. The story I must tell is of my Magickal trajectory. I poked around at this subject in former writings; I acknowledged the Witchy undercurrent with all my friends & associates, but never have I dealt with it head-on.

The reasons why are manifold. First, my education on these matters was stunted & neglected. Compared to the majority of humans, I might as well have been an expert. Yet compared to the true experts I was a novice of half-baked ideas & undisciplined logic. I was a pitifully unread wild card seeking mayhem upon the world with little thought as to what should manufacture its replacement. I simply did not know how to effectively garden, nor did I have any healthy seeds to plant.

Everything was chaos – not Chaos Magick, mind you – but raw, literal chaos. Truth is that I was so out of the loop, so pathetically uninformed, that I hadn't even heard of such a thing as Chaos Magick. Everything I knew came from other Witches I'd met, from movies & comic books – from beginner books of Buckland, Cunningham & the Farrar's – or the short-sighted, hedonistic writings of Anton Lavey.

At some point I just stopped searching. I was more preoccupied about living Witchcraft then reading it, because the entire point was the experience itself. The older I grew the more I left it on the backburner. Magick was always in mind and part of me, but bogged down by arrested development.

It wasn't until age 34 that anyone explained The Tree Of Life to me, or why it was relevant. Even then this person was imparting base knowledge from the Jewish perspective. That was all I knew of it – some Jewish thing, so why would it appeal to me at all? What business does a Witch who rejects all Abrahamic religions have in studying such a concept?

Once at age 17 I pulled Regardie's *Golden Dawn* off the bookstore shelf. All I saw was a confusing, over priced mammoth of a book filled with mystical Jewish stuff & Angel Magic. And that Tree Of Life thing once again, perplexing & calling to me although I had not the faintest idea why.

It was a brief conversation about The Tree Of Life with an enthusiastic young girl that opened the gates. Nearly a year later, my research led me to recognize Tarot Cards were educational flash cards for The Tree. I always thought Tarot was interesting, but not one person I ever encountered could tell me why they meant what they did or how it actually worked. No one had a blueprint – they were just reading whatever the tiny booklet said.

Well, as the story always goes, the serious Magick student upgrades the moment they recognize the fusion of Qabalah & Tarot. This is when the Magickian is truly born, and I am no different. See, I was a Witch, not a Magickian – simply because I didn't know what that title really meant. The High Magick of the Ceremonial Magicians & Magickians was off my radar, as was the concept that you can steal whatever you want from them and create your own practice. Witchcraft is a personal affair and Magick is the technology of imagination – use it to whatever ends necessary.

When I became enamored with Magick again at 34 I was happy in my simpleton world. I was returning to abandoned research from teenage days – *Scottish Witchcraft* by Buckland, *Drawing Down The Moon* by Adler. But then a series of dark events took place, and it all led to a mysterious Witch who was in town for a short time only.

She'd flown in her altar – a luggage case packed with trinkets & crystals & idols. In center of it all was a tiny plant that I touched foolishly when she'd left the room. She reentered and immediately noticed me puzzling over it: "*Don't touch that – it's Poison! It's from Aokihara!*" I had no idea what she was talking about, nor did I want to ask. I quickly washed my hands and forgot about it.

This will sound like whackadoo superstition, but extreme psychological duress began happening soon after touching that tree in the weeks & months that followed. Kooky as it may sound, it was like it poisoned me in a psychic sense. I considered that I was experiencing a nervous breakdown, but I could not help but question if that plant scrambled me in a lingering way. This Witch was only around for a short time and duly vanished, so there was no answer to its origin. But I knew that somehow I would figure out what that thing was.

Again, long backstory – linked to a gnarly childhood trauma, no less – but I'll just put it like this... For a number of strange reasons, I began investigating The Yew Tree. If you don't know what that is or why it is important, don't worry, I'll get there.

The Yew is a central historical item in the lore of Witchcraft, Magick, Paganism, Druidry, Vikings & The Occult that no one had ever wrote an expansive book, manual or Grimoire about. It was something that was everywhere in plain sight, just totally ubiquitous. It was titanic how widespread it was and an absolute shame that no one had ever pinpointed it for expansive discussion. Despite its massive importance, The Yew remained out of the loop for the modern Magick Community.

I began researching its intersection with Magick across world history. This gave my mind a solid platform to wrap my head around these topics and expand. It's what I'd been lacking – a central device to tie it all together.

It is The Yew which led me to Qabalah & Tarot unified, as I soon learned The Tree Of Life (and Qliphoth) is envisioned as a Yew. That Yggdrasil the Viking World Tree was a Yew and not an Ash, as modern research has shown. That The Yew was among The Druids most Holy Trees + its supreme connection to Celtic Samhain & Norse Yule. Plus its connection to so many major Pagan Deities. Odd to say, but without The Yew I would never be a Magickian today.

Of all jaw-dropping reveals, none hit harder then learning the plant that I felt had psychically poisoned me was of the Japanese Suicide Forest. Literally a living sample – a cutting from Aokihara, the "Sea of Trees" – a 13 square mile hallucinogenic Yew forest at the base of Mount Fuji. This was the cousin of the European Yew.

For whatever reason, the trees of the Suicide Forest give very bad trips. See, all Yews give off a hallucinogenic gas at certain temperatures; for whatever reason this forest brings on the nightmares. Endless stories of people committing suicide in the forest, hence its nickname – and tales of people "cursed" by handling the plants or touching the seeds. There were many anecdotes in the Magick Community of folks getting these trees, planting them, then offing themselves.

This Yew fascination overtook me, and for a year I obsessively prepared my findings into an 888 Page PDF Info-Comp which featured all the research I could muster – every Yew-infested corner of Paganism, Divinity, Witchcraft, Magick & the Infernal Divine. This is what led me to all corners of the Occult.

Halloween 2016 I aggressively dumped it on every social media platform as my gift to the Magick Community. Was it a Trick or a Treat? Well both, of course. As you may suspect, it turned out to be quite popular. People wrote from different corners of the planet saying that The Yew "chose me." *Ha!* Sure, why not? In any case, it was The Yew that unlocked the Occult for me. This is why my story is so different.

I am a variable that exists only because a long, freakish chain of events. Zeero Xiron is only so because of external factors – others made Magickal actions which disturbed the wildlife, and I am the Gander of Geese.

I always existed and would continue to exist as an individual – as Other Guy – but that fella was always a vehicle gestating an end result he didn't understand. Cluelessly onward he plodded through life unaware that a Zeero Xiron lurked within him. He pitifully did not know how to await the arrival of Zeero, hence he endlessly missed the boat.

Zeero Xiron is not a split personality; Z.X. is an upgrade. Will there be a further upgrade? Perhaps some day. For now it must be concluded two things. The man before (and Xiron as well) are both outcomes of Magickal actions that others had taken. The force & inertia with which they cast their spells into the world created damaging effects that fell, by proxy, upon the heads of both young Mr. Nobody and ol' Zeero Xiron.

Childhood Nobody wanted nothing to do with Witches at first – at least until age 8. For whatever reason, he just plainly didn't like them. But an awareness grew. One Saturday afternoon the rabbit eared TV was showing *Warlock* with Julian Sands. Watching the wizardly battle at the end of the film made him light up.

It just pulled a lever – he immediately could see the world with the eyes of the Witch. He went outdoors & called to the skies demanding they come alive. Grey clouds began storming & wind blowing (coincidence, of course) – he kept laughing & laughing. He was born with madness in his eyes and a monstrous grin on his face.

He willfully came to this path of his own volition and took it remarkably serious for someone so young whom had no teachers present, no internet, books or access to information. This was 1989, after all. And he was the product of a church going Irish Catholic family with whom he could never discuss his true beliefs.

Life went on. He drifted away, but by 34 dude made a Magickal comeback. His life became dedicated to Occult study; he wanted to teach to those who would listen. The issue was discovering his true voice...

And then across the Atlantic, in London, a psychopath Black Magickian stabbed to death 2 women in the park in a demonic pact attempt with Lucifuge Rofocale. This act and all the shockwaves it created rippled throughout the media, and more importantly, the global Magick community. Two women were dead by the hands of a delusional maniac who was directly inspired by a Magickal Grimoire this one big dumdum put out.

See, there's this Infomercial Satan Guy who used to be gigantic on YouTube before getting canceled & banned. For many years he ran his little book publishing / Ritual Service / merchandise pushing website, releasing an avalanche of questionable books unto the Magickal underground from multiple authors – material which was often "channeled" from the "Infernal Divine." His reach was gargantuan – *90,000 subscribers on YouTube!* He had cornered the market for the type of Black Magickian (and showman) that he was.

Problem is he ended up a cult leader. He didn't quite mean to, but that's where it led. He was claiming that the 9 Demonic Gatekeepers lived inside of him – that he could Infernally Bless you with them, demonically possess you with them, put you in touch with them so you can form your own pacts. And he was charging thousands of dollars for these services while pimping channeled books that also cost hundreds to buy.

He was like a Man-Lilith meets the Anti-Pope. He was an ex-Mormon refugee from that cult yet here he was starting another, and one of his followers bought this stupid book he released that gave all the steps for how to sacrifice a human to an imaginary demon to gain a pact for eternal riches & rewards. This crazy person actually followed the directions.

The BBC picked up the story – Sky News, Vice Magazine & FOX followed among a slew of other international media outlets. Satan Guy was cooked. He was abruptly banned from every social media platform he utilized. YouTube deleted all his videos – clear evidence that he was running a cult. If anything it was YouTube sweeping it under the rug to protect themselves from a class action lawsuit. *Just imagine the tech worker stumbling onto this psychosis!* Truth was his cancellation saved him.

This was an event that made Zeero and anyone involved with Magick look terrible. This is the kind of story that gets a new Satanic Panic going. Goofball played with fire and he scorched all of us by default. People could now identify us with him, just because they don't know any better.

The actions of this goomba threw a boulder into the lake, creating ripple effects to every corner of the Magick Community. It was the stink of it all that drifted into the nostrils of Doc Zeero. And so on a chill November evening, Xiron sat down outside a closed business in a barren factory section to have a long conversation with Infernal Empire Dude. Which was then aptly uploaded to YouTube.

Doc let him have it, like the ultimate bad Yelp review – like a phone message left in the middle of the night that went on for 2.5 hours. In one stroke, Dr. Zeero wandered up to The Hive of the Black Magick Mafia and just took a baseball bat to the hornet's nest. And thus Zeero Xiron was born to social media.

Other Guy had finally made it – *he'd successfully erased himself!* Like a computer program redesigned, Zeero Xiron (the upgrade) is the Finale of the Magickal Will, because the Magickal Identity is the Encoding of The Will. The old is cast aside...

What can be said of this forgotten character from whom Zeero sprang forth? Well, he was truly a character indeed. See, Mr. Nobody left behind 6 books and a number of secretive, widely circulated documents – plenty of music & journalism too. He had quite a career in the underground, slithering his way through the Metal, Punk, Industrial & EDM scenes.

Once upon a time he was something of a politician attempting to unite the different tribes. That was the essence of his glorious vision. Any artistic output was to aid that mission. For years he was a zealot.

The other manuscripts he'd produced – none tackle Magick so directly. The reason why is that when you write a tome about your own life – and you are dead serious about the Magickal Path – that Path itself deserves its own autobiography to parallel your normal life's tale. Nothing else can do it justice.

One day, when he was 35, Other Guy started to vanish. At the apex of his career, he simply ducked out. He had become an infamous character in many undergrounds and his music, books, art, message – they were circulating. For years he was getting press all over the world. Yet by 2016 he'd had his fill – enough was enough. As with so many of his other fateful decisions, he made a sudden impulse decision – *semi-retirement!* He had done what he set out to do and just wanted to live a private life.

Retreat would not be instantaneous but a slow, phased withdrawal. Even though it would ultimately take him a few years he began shutting down shop. Done with it all, long before 40 – the bands, the books, the touring, travel, webzines, magazines & newspapers. He stopped going to concerts or participating in any scene. Quit interacting with most anyone. He still had one last album to record and some shows to play, but during the process he ceased caring. March 2019 his Extreme Metal band broke up. In reaction, he went AWOL.

From thereon he was like a man curating a museum of his own works – he was his own press relations guy & record label person far removed from the fellow who had actually authored the books or performed the records. He'd grown so different then his old output that he was simply a caretaker of an estate.

As he continued to promote & release that which had long been completed, he shipped his books to libraries worldwide. His "retirement" was managing a money pit of free promo items sent every direction of the compass. But you know what? It worked. There he sits on the library shelves of Harvard, Yale, Princeton and countless other Major Cities & Universities. He did what he set out to do then turned away, enthusiastic to fully lunge into the realms of Magick & The Occult.

The driving force that once propelled him recalibrated to examine his internal plane. Spiritual & Psychological Alchemy was evolving of its own accord. His Witchy roots called to him, but he sought more. Where he once sought chaos – to upend reality & warp it into his own twisted image – he now sought harmony.

In his younger days he stood for nothing more then laughing at burning things with eyes ablaze. He was a wily trickster, inspired by Loki & others. He was the snake in the garden of his youth offering apples & coercing teenagers into Witchcraft & Satanism like a lurking Goblin creature in an 18th Century German Woodcut. But this kid, he was rudimentary – all about psychic energy manipulation, telepathy & telekinesis; psychic vampirism, ghosts, deja vu, shared dreams, intuitive power...

By May 2017 he was evicted and went permanently mobile – living in a van for the next several years, most of every paycheck going to free copies of books sent to libraries & reviewers. By 2020 that mission had concluded; he was saving up to rent an apartment. He was finally going to set up his little Witchy lair and make incense from scratch, guerrilla garden the city, dramatically promote Magick with free books, fliers, brochures.

One paycheck away and Covid hit hard; he was laid off, the world crumbled, and soon he was isolated in a band rehearsal space for 8 months & sleeping outside every night in a warehouse district. By Thanksgiving 2020 he was nearly broke and forced to hit the street, living in a tent in the railyard the entire winter.

By May 2021, he had found a parking lot to pop a tent where he remained until Dr. Zeero Xiron was finally born. From thereon, everything was on an upswing. He had found his New Voice and was ecstatic. But then the poor bastard suddenly went schizophrenic. He was led to the Psych Ward and there he stayed for nearly 2 weeks, unsure of who he was or what reality consisted of. In a funk of exhaustion & mania, he simply collapsed into madness.

Mr. Nobody eventually snapped out of it, but a good chunk of the man he was before had passed away in that spell of insanity. His brain never quite worked again as it had before. What was spit out of the Psych Ward was a broken mess held together by psychiatric medication masking an unpredictable mental illness.

One day he was sharp as a tack, the next his brain took him to an alternate universe for a month. The remnants slowly coagulated into the shape of Zeero Xiron, although it wasn't totally clear even then. It all just kind of happened. The Magickal identity subsumes the mundane. Zeero now writes these words, and that is fine by me.

For this manuscript to continue, there must be a sudden recognition of two realities – just what is the intelligence behind these words, and what is the meaning of this Magick it professes? For Magick, anyone involved will tell you something similar yet different, because it is ultimately custom tailored in regards to their own worldview.

Other Guy and Xiron, what can be said of them? Zeero, at least on social media, was always presented as an asexual voice in space. His face and gender were totally unimportant. But what of the real man behind the facade? He and Zeero weren't always the same. They just slowly morphed together until there was one alchemized being.

Well, the truth is that Zeero Xiron is asexual out of choice. This obviously wasn't always the case. That rapscallion had many relationships & encounters, but one day, he began looking at trees the way he once looked at women. It's like his entire attraction to the human race was replaced by nature itself. He did a total 180 – he was a creature of the city & horny little devil turned asexual elemental vampire juicing off the trees.

Yet he was once a very sexual person. In his late 20's he had come to terms with his pansexual nature, although he was never truly comfortable with it or successful at it. Technically, he could be romantic or physical with anyone regardless of gender. He was selectively attracted to very few people, to the point where he hardly noticed anyone at all. He also wore baggy clothes as not to attract attention.

The outside world told him he was handsome, yet he shied away from prying eyes. He was always buried beneath a hoodie & aggressive looking clothes, hidden behind sunglasses & hats. All too often they gave him the nickname "The Unibomber."

His ability to be attracted to others withered over time until he had become extremely demisexual. He had to really know someone well to actually grow attraction, and his affairs were always quite private and took a long time to gestate.

He couldn't just pick up someone at the bar after talking for 20 minutes and jump in the sack. In his younger days he was open to such a thing, but the older he became, the less he wanted anyone to touch him. Furthermore, as a Magickal type, he was heavily psychic. It was always a big deal to get physical. You cross streams.

After openly coming out as bisexual (the concept of pansexuality was not in his vocabulary back then) he really wanted a relationship with another male. He worked frustratingly hard to make it occur – emptiness constantly reaching out to nothingness.

Nothing romantic ever happened on that end. He had drifted all over the USA & Europe seeking someone, anyone at all. Years of effort only amounting to unsatisfactory one night stands or situations that might last a few days at best, ending pathetically.

Furthermore, he downright detested 90% of men and was only attracted to maybe 7% of them. Good luck making both percentages key up! He also just plainly did not resonate with gay culture. He was friendly but lost with that crowd. He was not a man of rainbow flags, shorty shorts, limp wrists or corny lisps.

He was the no frills working man type, gravitating to places where people listened to Led Zeppelin, wore leather jackets, watched movies like *Die Hard*, rode Harley's and shot billiards all night. If they weren't toned & manly, he simply wasn't interested. Good luck that any of them could remotely live up to his expectations though.

More often then not, he would hang out at gay bars constantly yet everyone would just assume he was straight and not even bother to engage with him. It was flabbergasting – why would a straight guy hang out at gay bars all the time? Why would a straight person want to work at gay bars for years? He was just as confused by them all as they were of him.

Still, despite people constantly telling him he was making it all up for some unknown purpose, he refused to give up on this notion that he was likely "all the way gay" and simply never found his match. Anytime he got close, either they weren't reciprocal or it went awry. He never had a relationship with another male last more then a week, despite actively trying since 2009. Still, it was clear to him that whenever he was seriously interested, he was far more attracted to them then any woman.

Compounding the situation, Other Guy had an S&M streak that was totally unexplored. There was much he was willing to do but just like all factors of his love life he was left unsatisfied, inexperienced, perpetually awkward.

This sadomasochistic streak would continue until he eventually decided none of it was truly natural to him and that he didn't want any of it in his life anymore. He knew it was a forced thing anyway that was pushed on him in the first place. It had soiled his life and plagued all his relationships & interactions. It was a curse, not an enthusiasm. And what is the use engaging in intimacy if no enthusiasm exists?

Also, it has to be stated that while he enjoyed that his default form was male, he had no allegiance to it whatsoever. He often felt like a thing and not a person, and gender was simply another idea. Had he the ability, he would snap his fingers and turn into a beautiful woman just to have the experience of doing so. But he would also snap his fingers and turn into a shark or a dragon.

Sometimes he felt a strong womanly vibe, other times he felt very male. Then there were times where he felt a perfect union of both or simply neither – at times he felt a genderless alien intelligence piloting a body that just happened to be male.

He did not care enough about these experiences to cross dress or consider hormone therapy or surgery. He was fine being seen as a default male, and it was really no one's business anyway. He didn't care what anyone thought of how he felt inside. Just like Magick, it was personal.

In consideration of these factors, he'd long ago left the predominantly straight worlds of Heavy Metal & Punk Rock & the general bar scene. He preferred to exclusively hang out in the gay scene. He wanted to be around people like himself, even if he had little in common with them outside the meat & potatoes of the whole issue.

He'd rather avoid the angry straight people, even if he was technically the angry queer man at the bar. They were always friendly until they got to know him because he was poster boy for their disdain – dirty Punk Rock guy nutcase protester person pushing creepy Witchcraft stuff & conspiracy talk. They would never accept him, just as he felt dejected from the Metal and Punk crowds.

Mr. Nobody was a person from a Punk Rock ethos. He worked tirelessly promoting bands, booking shows, aiding the Punk Community + the Industrial, Metal & EDM folks any way he could. But when opening up to his sexuality, the rumblings of *"F**k you faggot"* were underway.

Even if both scenes had plenty of smiling faces, the hecklers were in the background. It's one thing to be Rob Halford, it's another to be some local guy playing death metal at a dive bar. It's also one thing for someone to hear you have homosexual tendencies, it's another to factor in sadomasochism. People go from uncomfortable & squirming to just wanting to flee the room instead.

He knew he could no longer be a leader of any sort. People mocked him behind his back and told all kinds of lies. Antifa kids accused him of being a secret racist Nazi sympathizer and spread such fabrications. Others claimed he was a disreputable Black Magick Witch that had to be stopped. Some pushed the narrative that he was a Straight Cis Male S&M psychopath looking to sexually beat up all the females.

People just bought into it without question. No one would confront him. All he ever wanted was for hot chicks to kick his ass anyway. *He was the one who wanted to get beat up!* He never felt right getting rough with a female. In fact, many of his ex-girlfriends had abandoned him because he wouldn't get hardcore S&M on them. He was inept.

Others just downright didn't like the looks of him, or felt threatened by his sheer vibe. Some thought he was another person who had the same last name, who had long ago got himself canceled before Mr. Nobody ever moved to town. Everyone thought he was this guy yet no one would ever say a thing to him about it! For years people were telling each other not to help or aid him in any way – to not book his bands, to not buy or read his books, to sabotage him at every turn – *all because they thought he was someone else!*

The shit storm of haters continued – they assassinated one of their best & brightest, having been herded like a mob by a handful of people. Either because they were jealous of him, threatened by him or that he simply refused to have sex with people who creepily stalked him.

Despite this avalanche of feces they attempted to bury him alive with, he stood up and let his presence be known. All that time he kept a low profile. He didn't want the scenesters to know who he really was or just how widely he was known in the outside world. Portland was the place where he tried to be an anonymous nobody.

But finally, they caught on. With shocked faces they realized who they had gone to war with. Shaking off their arrows and removing the daggers from his back, he stood up like a colossus. He dropped book after book, album after album. He wasn't a local Big Fish, he was a Global Leviathan. They simply could not stop him.

Most importantly he would get his revenge – he'd tear through their city with Magick, turn all of their girlfriends into Witches. The city would be rendered into a 100,000 strong Coven! And then all those loser males with no Magickal inclination – no one would ever hump them again. *Moo ha ha!* He would dry up that Pussy Well like the blaze of the Sahara, engineer a Pagan freakout so intense Portland's image would be on par with Salem.

The 888 page *Book of Yew* was his mad attack. He always said he was going to do something special for the kids on Halloween. That year, 2016, he put out not only The Yew manuscript, but his magnum opus autobiography with worldwide distribution...

5 months afterwards his house folded; it was the end of the road for basement concert houses. Shortly before eviction his long time on again / off again girlfriend was found dead – floating in the river, likely murdered while hitchhiking Oregon. Something in him died with her. He could barely process it; it was just like an event that happened and he couldn't emotionally connect to it...

Everything had gone wrong. The great Metal/Punk dream had collapsed into being the reviled janitor at a drunk punk kid party house. He was cursed or ignored by this crop of youth far from what was once home, totally segregated from anyone involved in his long history of playing music, throwing shows, being a community helper. He was 35 and felt 60; an old man surrounded by young kids who no longer understood a thing he was saying, all of whom eyeballed him like a snake.

It was time to move on and just become what he always was – underground writer guy putting out fringe books, free to travel anywhere in the world he pleased, forever on tour because all he ever needed to be on tour was a laptop and his own voice and to simply show up somewhere. With a pen & paper, he could make miracles happen.

Although he could have vanished on some DIY tour, he decided to go mobile – the constant van life of a Portland home bum, living like a pirate from block to block inside a vehicle. Until the cops make us leave, this is our new home. Each city block was always good for about a week, then knock knock goes the policeman. *"Scram, beat it."* No problem chief – onto the next block...

It went on like this for years. It was just Other Guy, a black cat, and a strange autistic girl reading comic books & watching cartoons & Pro Wrestling as he methodically launched his book publishing company. Simple as the situation was, it's all he ever really wanted. Together they were researching & exploring Magick, messing with Tarot cards, collecting crystals – simpleton Witch stuff.

Even while homeless in a van, still he played in his final band – an extreme metal project. After a dozen shows & one solid album, the band folded in March 2019. He spent the rest of that year releasing the unpublished book of his youth – something he withheld for 15 years waiting for the right moment. He always said the second he put it out the world would end. Once the final promo copy was mailed out, Covid exploded. This is when the story completely goes to hell...

Covid destroyed America. The Street had never been more Street, and the Inside never more Inside. Into this inferno he plunged – homeless in a new world with new rules & challenges. It was never more apocalyptic or end of the line for him.

He would remain homeless all the way until February 2023. Securing a room & decent job, he returned to the world & met some solid people. He could be found at any of the gay bars doing free Tarot readings, handing out incense sticks, candles & comic books. For the very special, he'd hand out the finest Witchcraft & Magick books just to get the chain reaction going. Because Magick always begins with one seed planted...

But then they pulled the chair out from under his ass again, kicked him to the street in August 2024. After a rough stretch of boiling sun & urban camping, by September he'd found housing... And here Zeero Xiron now is, perplexed, unsure where this is all heading – swallowed by the Fascist dictatorship of President Chump & a country wildly divided...

Those unfamiliar with the term Magick, who vaguely think of Witches on brooms or cloaked figures casting spells in Pentagram fueled rituals, will not understand what is meant by this word when a figure like Zeero Xiron prattles it out. An abstract notion this "Magick" certainly is; the uninformed onlooker will only see a confusing blob of people.

Fat chance they will know the difference between any archetype. All of these names will be foreign to them, their figures blurred – Magus, Druid, Witch, Shaman, Sage, Magician, Sorcerer, Alchemist, Magickian, Oracle. Some will heckle their very existence, others will fear or disdain them claiming they worship The Devil.

Magick, despite how simple it is, eludes a unanimous definition. Anyone who practices it will give you a different, yet similar, response. It goes something like this – Magick is the art & science of managing cause & effect by means of magnetism & willpower merged with the imagination, mind, body, spirit & Universe itself.

Using the full faculties of ones intellect & psychic prowess, a virile force of willpower is pushed into the open world. It is this very force traveling from Point A (the practitioner) to Point B (the target) which best explains "Magick." It is the outpouring force of an individual, encoded with all the necessary information & psychic power needed to manipulate the target in question.

Anything else deemed "Magick" has to do with the dynamics of the inner plane and the energies of the individual in the quest for spiritual refinement & self mastery. That which is deemed "Magickal" are additions to these basic principles – such as techniques or systems.

Thus, there are countless Magickal traditions in world history, all which claim differing worldviews & paradigms. The Magick of one is not the Magick of another – but the force of Magick works for all. The real question is what side do you stand on?

The Magick community is fractured. That's just what happens with an entire culture based on zealous faith in the self. The entire point is the evolution of the individual, and no ascensions can occur mimicking an other's path. Your path is unique and it is a crooked one full of pitfalls, wrong turns, overgrown foliage & calamities.

Magick is fanatical – it turns you into a living ritual 24-7. The outside world won't recognize it, but one must understand that Magick to us is as dead serious as a heart attack with flames in its eyes. Magick is life or death – even when it's tongue is firmly in cheek.

Furthermore, we have to chat about Dr. Zeero and his place in the Grand Game of Chess all of us Magickal folks are playing with each other by default. Another analogy is the good old game of Poker. Hell, even *Magic: The Gathering* is appropriate, but upon the battleground of our lives. Because whether or not you chose to participate with others in Magick, the others are already including you by proxy. Just by practicing Magick as a solo act you are inevitably drawn into our worldwide Game.

In an underground of wildly different attitudes, worldviews, paradigms, ideas of evolution & ascent, there are, of course, certain divisions. You have White Magick vs. Black Magick and the Greys in-between, plus you have the Right Hand Path vs. Left Hand Path and this ideological war is forever raging. This is all Magickian talk, of course – Witches seldom get wrapped up in this RHP / LHP argument. Witches & Druids often prefer the Green. But then you have the Chaos Magicians as well, many of whom refuse to claim any side.

Then you have Zeero Xiron. What Ash was versus *The Evil Dead*, here you have another foul-mouthed, wise cracking, middle finger waving psycho battling the Armies of Darkness. This is the beauty of the Dr. Zeero Xiron Free Magick Secrets Show. Doc isn't a Mega Troll, he is a Social Media Superstar with a mouth the size of Uranus.

Doc warns his flock on the dangers of the Left Hand Path. While not necessarily at war with anyone on a personal level, he is certainly at war with many of the bad ideas that gurgle from their lips like the raw sewage of a broken sewer main.

Despite his luminous high-fallutin' hyperbole, there have been times where Doc has blatantly turned heel as if a Pro Wrestler. Doc Zeero has often gone from noble communicator teaching esoteric wisdom to Magickal Supervillain on the drop of a dime.

It must be noted that Other Guy always played the role of Supervillain throughout life. The second he read his first comic book, his mind was made up. Throughout life his antisocial personality was nearly totalitarian. He grew up one twisted, alienated, violent, isolated kid who rejected nearly everyone. If he didn't like or respect you, you were canon fodder or pawns.

That Witchcraft & Satanism & the Occult blossomed among the youth of the 90's only increased his mad Magickal plans and launched his ego into space, turning him into a freakish dictator of his own self-willed Empire.

It has already been stated the sort of things he preached, but it again must be underscored what a troublemaker he truly was, and how dismal his Magickal projection – mayhem for mayhem's sake. He was a full-on Gremlin. It was only after he was spanked by the cumulative result of all his turgid Magickal deeds that he changed.

He was a much different man by the time he finally climbed onto social media as Dr. Zeero. Yet even so, despite his well meaning promotion of Spiritual & Psychological Alchemy, Doc still wants to cook 'em all a stew they'll choke on.

The world he envisions and his idea of God runs counter to everything so many believe that he is ultimately rendered The Snake of all their religions. He truly is that dark tempter the religious folks warn their children about. Doc Zeero lurks upon their flock, coaxing Mormon girls into Witchcraft and seducing Catholic girls into masturbating to Satan. This is when he knows he has won...

Let it be known that there are different classes of Supervillains. See, there are flawed yet sympathetic types, Anti-Hero Adversaries & True Monsters. What is meant by "flawed yet sympathetic" is that the driving motive is sympathetic yet warped enough to be dangerous, usually based on psychological reaction to some unfortunate event. A True Monster, however, is a non negotiable tyrant with no redeeming value.

The Anti-Hero Adversary is only a Supervillain if one chooses to recognize as such. This is the class that Dr. Zeero belongs to. See, what is right for me is not right for the world at large; I am the adversary of the masses. The global vision I emit runs counter to the vast majority of humankind and I am no doubt their Devil.

It is Doc's opinion that none of these phony religions in man's history remotely serve the one True God, or better stated, the One True Architect of Creation. Trust me, that thing is a riddle you will never get to the bottom of. So Monotheism it is, the supreme source above all. As above, so below – you are the Macrocosm by virtue of the gift of intelligence.

But how can one be a Supervillain and a zealot of the one True God? Because it harnesses a viewpoint that to see with the eyes of the True God, humanities self assured delusions and illusions are blown to bits. To align yourself with The Creator is to become an abnormal agent deconstructing all the illusions that mankind holds dear. The more holy you become the more anarchist you are rendered.

But the world I envision has much more to it then the conception of God. It is the entire upheave of human society and its reorganization that I fight for. To impose willpower in this sense to enact your wild vision and make it reality – you must essentially become a dictator of your own ideology. Your physical body becomes your state territory. You must dictate this terrain with an iron fist. You must be self authoritarian.

In this sense, what is Satanism but a reflection of self nationalism & self empire? At least in the whole "Satan as a symbol and not a theistic reality" sense. And how could anyone into Theistic Satanism not view themselves as a Supervillain anyway? Dictators of their own spiritual journey, deranged scribes of their own mischievous manifestos. See, it doesn't take much to be a Supervillain.

The world Zeero Xiron envisions runs so counter to the world as it stands that his triumph would be an apocalypse of sorts for the common man. To force billions to live his vision would be a cruel enforcement. Not that his vision is cruel – it is simply that what is right for him is not correct for anyone else.

My name is Zeero Xiron and I am a real life Supervillain. I don't have friends, I have henchmen. If they are another Supervillain with a truce – that's a difference. Otherwise they work for me, because everyone works for me.

I am a gangster, I'm an anarchist; I'm a propagandist, a pirate, I am a criminal and I am an adversary. You Left Hand Path kids worship Satan, but I am Satan. You have no idea the mind speaking these words. I'm not here to build community, I'm here to warp the world in my own twisted image & delete the whole of human culture that I detest.

I'm not Right or Left Hand Path – I am the super-ego which supersedes both options. I am not striving to ascend to Godhead assimilation or follow the Qliphotic sewers into supposed self Godhood. I am a Supervillain and the game is mine. I roll the nickels, I paint the dice. And I'm here for one purpose – to transform every man, woman and child into a Supervillain too. Plus the entire gamut of genders.

See, I'm sick of henchmen, I want none to exist. I am an engineer of souls. I seek to lead all of humanity straight into the padded cells of Arkham Asylum & I'm here to turn every city on the globe into Gotham. Why? Because it's our playground. We are the lost children and our game is most fun. In the chaos we now step forward; in the shadows we do our work...

Despite my raging brouhaha, there is a lighter side to this Anti-Hero Adversary. My practice has molded & mutated over time. You know, I started out a simple Witch. Ended up a Magickian by default but one of my own weird brand where a lot of seemingly contradictory things are going on.

At one end I'm like a simpleton Witch that wants to fuse with nature, on the other end there's this Ceremonial Magickian guy in me that strives to gain gnosis with the Godhead. Not to be absorbed by it but to understand it, in order to know both halves of God.

See, there is The Creation & The Creator – both are halves which unify a whole. It is the ALL that I seek fusion with – everything The Universe is and everything outside of it as well. My quest is not to be reabsorbed but to seek immortality as a Heretic Ipsissimus in gnosis with The Creation. I do not care what lay beyond the boundaries of physical existence other then to understand what it is. I am fine in the sea of the cosmos exactly where I am.

To be an Ipsissimus you "hang around," so to speak. You become a function of the physical universe and a mind cruising its intergalactic highways forever (theoretically). What makes me the heretic of them all is I reject the fusion of the Holy Guardian Angel – something I just don't trust and poo poo on the concept of.

I'm obsessed with Creation & Creator at the same time. And I'm Monotheist, basically, but just the idea of one Architect / one Creation. Essentially I'm promoting both a total gnosis with The Architect but equally important gnosis with Creation.

They say you are going in two separate directions at the same time, how is that possible? On negates the other. How can you split your focus? Well, isn't that part of being a Magickian and what Magick teaches? To split your focus in all manner of ways while remaining a unified whole? I feel like it's all One Big Thing.

Now, I keep mentioning Witchcraft specifically. Because old habits die hard and I'll never let that idea go. So even though I want to go as deep into nature as I possibly can, I just learned to view the entire universe as nature.

Witchcraft is an earth centered nature religion based upon what physically exists. My concept of nature had gone from the flora & lakes & sands & sky to expanding to the very boundaries of the universe. And if that isn't mind expansion I don't know what is. So the only way to put it is the term "Cosmic Witchcraft."

Above all, I promote what has been called "Elemental Vampirism." You're not a vampire sucking their psychic energy – Elemental Vampirism is when you are juicing off the forces of nature surrounding you. It's a complete union...

Cosmic Witchcraft is a simple thing to wrap your head around. The Microcosm is a tool at our disposal. It is ours for the taking and manipulation thereof. Intellectually, spiritually – any & all techniques. We are Creators inside The Creation.

"Made in The Image of The Creator" – you are the Microcosm of the Macrocosm. If God created you in Its image then the only answer would be your own God in terms of The Creation itself. If the imagination and willpower are the two driving forces of the individual – and if you are the doppelganger of The Creator – then what is the use of fighting against it? You don't want to sound self righteous and say God is on your side, but you can say the laws of the universe are on your side, because you are God and A God as well.

Cosmic Witchcraft, naturally, is obsessed with the Wheel Year and observing the 8 High Days of Magick. It is essential bedrock. Pantheism is still allowable even if one is Monotheist – all of the Gods & Goddesses are all symbols, totems, archetypes. Ways to create avatars in our mind to represent forces of nature or psychologies or psychological processes. They have their function – it's OK to ritualize them. But I don't believe in them as real entities – more like thought forms with a life of their own that you animate.

Is it possible that we all share a collective unconscious and we are all psychically hooked to each other? That these Deities are just shared archetypes fusing all known data somehow coagulating into one specific mental egregore that communicates back? Again, pseudoscience & superstition – but maybe not? It's hard to overlook all the experiences humans have had throughout their development. If even one of these stories is true, then it proves the reality of these functions.

The Gods live as egregores we create from our shared experience on this so called "Astral Plane." And what is this Astral Plane, if it indeed exists? Certainly a channel of shared collective unconscious. Ants have antennae to communicate – humans have the pineal gland. Just because we don't have appendages outside our skulls does not negate we have the same prowess the insect does. We simply cannot measure it scientifically. If you ask me, it's a central feature why certain forms of Magick actually works.

I don't believe in Heaven or Hell, I don't believe in karma or reincarnation or the Wiccan "Rule of 3." I think when people ritually summon Deities by evoking / invoking they are creating avatars in their own mind so they can communicate with otherwise hidden aspects of themselves by forming a powerful mind symbol which can reply to a querent or seeker. Suggestion is a powerful thing.

Doc will never put his seal of approval on if demons or angels are real – ghosts, djinn, whatever. Perhaps an invisible plane exists where such creatures could tangibly occur? They have their own laws governing them, supposedly. It is a strange universe we barely understand, so why not this possibility? Doc knows not how to access this invisible world but does not totally discount it either. Regardless, Xiron warns to be skeptical of any Occult practitioner who claims to wield The Secret.

Unlike Eliphas Levi, Aleister Crowley or Golden Dawn members – I reject the Holy Guardian Angel. I advise against it. But fusion with The Higher Self? Yes. You want to say Holy Guardian Angel as representative of The Highest Self – then yes.

On the Infernal side, extreme caution must also be practiced. If you're a person performing rituals & attempting communications with Lilith or Lucifer or Belial or Azazel or whoever – just because something shows up and tells you it's Belphegor does not make it so. You're talking about a vampiric, psychic leech. *"Wow look at this Black Magician Yahoo"* it would think to itself – *"better just tell him I'm Abaddon and have him do my bidding."*

How else would such an entity look upon a Left Hand Path Black Magickian? Some guy having a ritual in a self made temple stuffed with burning candles & incense, slicing himself and bleeding on demonic sigils just beckoning these forces to come to him. What else would a vampiric entity think other then: *"there's a sucker born every minute?"*

Ritual in so many aspects is about opening yourself up to an invisible world and becoming its medium. The trick is to find the balance of being guarded while acting as an open floodgate. Hence the obsession with protective circles and such. But like everything else, it's just another prop to make your mind feel secure.

Understand that all the classic Witchy items are just props used to somehow flick on the light in your head & make the psychic process happen. I love all the props – the altar, the idols, the human skulls & crystal balls – but Magick is about Mind Power which requires only the individual.

Want to be the strongest? Just sail into nature butt naked under the full moon in the dead of night, howling like a wolf alone in the forest, batshit crazed from psychedelic mushrooms, building a fire from rubbing twigs & dancing around the bonfire totally out of your mind. That's the essence of Witchcraft. You don't need the Athame & three legged table & crystal collection & organite & radionics boxes. All that shit is just for play, toys to get your mind to the place it needs to be. Stripped of all, you find your power.

When you think in a Monotheist way it ties into a lot of Hermetic & Qabbalistic ideas – like the anarchist version the Zohar. The Tree Of Life & Divine Emanations & all the Pythagorean number Magick that ties into it – this is all a wonderful way of mapping out the energies of The Universe in the Microcosm / Macrocosm sense.

Nothing teaches you how to fuse with the shadows & natural rhythms of The Universe more then you'll find in The Ninja. As well as the Esoteric Buddhist ideas flourishing in Ninpo plus Mountain Ascetic practices. Ninja philosophy, discipline, tactics, mind control – if it wasn't for the Ninja I wouldn't be who I am today. And that doesn't even have to do with fighting techniques. It's the picture as a whole, the lucid structure of it.

I also must mention Aikido. The power dynamics of how it works, how you never injure your opponent. How you disarm someone by constantly using their own inertia from them. I took everything I could learn from the *Art of Peace* by Morihei Ueshiba and the aesthetic of Aikido to redirect my own thoughts, to calm my own issues.

I've also studied *Art of War* by Sun Tzu and both of these books are complementary to each other. It is integral to think in terms of both at once; to put any plan you have through all your analyzable techniques with both hemispheres of thought in mind. It's important to analyze things from the standpoint of both in order to achieve a correct balance.

Now, in terms of Magickal growth – you may start out something else and become something else entirely, because all the different traditions you encounter end up changing your own tradition. You should be forming your own tradition anyway.

I started out a humble Witch, booby trapped by Magicians & Catholic Witches (long story). Witchcraft gave way to Satanism, which gave way to Paganism. Witchcraft went dormant, Magick remained. Without understanding it, I had in spirit become a Chaos Magickian. Embroiled in the Bardic phase of my as yet unknown Druid journey. I graduated, in notion, to Ovate.

By the time I was 34 all of this was background, but stunted & neglected – but then the great Magickal reawakening came. First as Witch & Pagan, but thirsting for knowledge. I soon reached what I had become – a Druid of the 3rd class, the Master Druid; the beginning of that journey with heavy emphasis on trajectory.

But then I found Qabalah & The Tree Of Life – I was irreparably faced with the path of the Ceremonial Magician (and eventually Magickian). Like so many before me I had walked onto the path of the Magus and of Alchemy. The truth though was that I represented a radically different form. Rejecting the Holy Guardian Angel I became what can only be described as a Heretic Magus.

I tried to dig my hands back into The Earth and its system of roots, reclaim the focus of The Moon. *"Witches of Earth, climb higher then Malkuth,"* said the inner voice. Earthy Witchcraft had expanded to the very boundaries of The Universe – The ALL was The Divine, not simply The Goddess, Sun, Moon or Sky Father. All Deities, Angels & Daemons had their place as faces of nature – psychological representations of the inner plane. They were all valid yet ultimately inconsequential. The Grand Trump was the ALL.

Like a dragon that's wings are made of The Tree Of Life and Tree of Death you fly with both as the Monad of your own personal universe. Your Will becomes the central point in space. You are both your own God and in synch with quote/unquote God. The highest form of gnosis comes as a result of the contradictory seeming ceremony of opposites.

God lives with God dead, for you are both God of one universe and an inconsequential speck in another. In the Tarot, remain The Fool. In the playing cards, remain The Joker. Yet all throughout I played the role of the Shaman. The overarching goal of all gnosis therefore is to arrive the Heretic Ipsissimus...

All of this would be garbled nonsense had I read it at the very beginning of my journey. And despite everything, I long to remain an ignorant, simplified Witch. With the Sun and Moon as the Eyes of God and my hands firmly entrenched in the soil, the roots, the rocks. For supreme vision and its attainment, one must exemplify & absorb the Alpha and Omega simultaneously with the mid-point of both as the eternal balance.

I'm a Heretic Ninja because I don't do physical discipline. I'm a Heretic Magickian because I reject the Holy Guardian Angel. I'm a Heretic Witch because I'm talking about Monotheism. But I'm also a Heretic Druid because I subsume their structure & notion while distancing myself from Celtic mythology. I deny their belief in the Otherworld – something all historical Druids preached.

The point of Druidry these days is you are a "jack of all trades" at service to the Pagan community at large. You move through the tribes like a politician & priest combined. Being a teacher, a builder, a crisis worker, psychologist, therapist, exorcist, alchemist, lecturer, consultant and Witch Doctor while assuming priestly functions. The role of the Druid is a taxing, wide ranging one of noble pursuit. You have to be a special kind of character to be a Druid; you must have that priestly air about you.

Now, being a Druid Supervillain adds another layer to the whole thing. In a soft sense, Heretic Druidry is when you hijack the Druid notion and warp it to your own specifications. There's also ways to be a Druid Supervillain and to culturally appropriate the Druid dynamic towards your Supervillain Masterplan.

Druids had 3 classes. You had to study for 20+ years and then you were a Master Druid. In the interim period you start out a Bard – you're like a musician / poet and learn the Druidic lessons bit by bit. Eventually you graduate to being an Ovate, which is like a diviner or seer – the Witch Doctor / Shaman guy of the bunch. The proper Druid was the dude – the boss of all 3 classes.

Cultural appropriation is fine because we're Supervillains, we do whatever the f**k we want. We just take it – that's the whole point, you know. All this dibble dabble about cultural insensitivity, this shit goes right out the window. It's a free for all. Being a Supervillain means never having to say you're sorry.

That's why Chaos Magick is the preferred Magickal ethos of the Supervillain Magickian. It's totally cool with cultural appropriation, it's cool with stealing anything in the history of Magick and using it for ones own ends. So take a little Chaos Magick, a sprinkle of Supervillain Manifesto and mix it up with the Druid notion. Why not?

Think of it like this – the henchmen are the Bards, the Ovates are the Mini-Bosses, the Druid is the Supervillain proper at the head of the organization You could have an Arch Druid but, you know, Supervillains – there isn't quite a Supervillain International yet, and we don't need one either, because being a Supervillain is being independent. It's being a lone wolf more often then not.

When you're a Supervillain of Doc Zeero's breed, and when you're an oldschool Monotheist Magician type – that doesn't really align with historical Druidry. Cause here's the thing – The Druids weren't a religion, they were overseers of all the different religions. They were like utilitarian priestly figures officiating things. It's kind of a blank, which is good.

To be a Supervillain Druid, you would therefore be facilitating all the other Supervillains out there. You would be their priestly sort of figure. Their handyman, their go-to. You can dump all the hitched mythology, all the Celtic jibber jabber. What you assume is solid program. And this is what Druidry has to offer.

Once you put yourself in the driver seat of your Supervillain Chariot, anything can happen. Because when you roll as a Supervillain, the world is your oyster…

In Dreams I Walk With Yew

Into the accursed night I raised my fist & shouted to The Gods: "*Where is my wife?!?*" I slammed my fist onto the table, as if the Magickal pounding of Mjölnir wrought with frustration, emptiness & unfulfillment. I felt electrical shockwaves fly in every direction as if I had called out to all Spirits, Ghosts, Entities & Ancestors – if my Partner indeed walks the Earth, I Will The Universe to bring her to me.

Immediately a "ding" notification on my laptop – the dating site OkCupid. Puzzled, I found a Witch messaging me fresh to town. She was mighty sultry & dark as the deep woods; we'd scored a 99.99% compatibility rating. This was significant because that summer Dr. Zeero had answered at least 3000 personality questions; anyone walking The Earth scoring so identical seemed a fiction.

This is coming in the wreckage of the most healthy relationship I ever had. All Summer I'd been with what many may describe as a "normal person." I was hopelessly infatuated with her as well as The Exit she represented. But it was bound to collapse from the get-go – I was 34, she 23. Wanted to keep her forever but it wasn't in The Cards. Eventually she shot me down – it wasn't malicious, it just had to end.

I was heartbroken & thrust in rebound to chasing the main "type" of my younger days – Black Magick Momma whom I could gladly be the Voodoo Doll of. Or at least it seemed that's what I should be doing – Nothing But Trouble, just how I liked it. But the truth was that Normy had introduced me to the lighter side of things, and I'd considerably changed.

I agreed to meet this mysterious date. My mind was alight with Witchy Business – I was looking to play The Game as aggressively as ever. I had no way of understand just how critical this meeting was to the trajectory of my life. And it's not even about her – it's just what she exposed me to in the brief week that I knew her.

Back then, I didn't care about "Magickal Hygiene." That's when you get tainted for messing around with a stanky aura. Merging with someone sexually "crosses the streams" – you infect each others' psychic being. You don't want to mess with anyone remotely connected to the Infernal Divine or you adopt some of their hellish baggage. All of their psychic energy – it's like rust & dry rot. On come the maggots.

Zeero Xiron is such a far cry from this person being written about that to retrace the steps just seems pitiful. There is a code of conduct now in physical intimacy. Magick is dead serious on many fronts – and it also redesigns the dating game & "private time."

The thing that prevents Dr. Zeero from dating another male is that they have no place of function in his invasion of Witchcraft Covens & Magickal Orders. To be like a Magistellus to Pilgrims, Zeero must lurk upon Christian women and convert them to Witchcraft & Paganism. It's his whole concept of a scoreboard – freeing their minds & souls one by one. In the shadows he glides, emerging from the darkness offering Witchy books, Tarot packs & comic books to young women wandering the foggy streets at night.

The gay scene isn't really down with such antics – they find it creepy. Well no shit, it is creepy – that's the whole point. It's the creepiest thing he could ever think of doing, as is why he does it. Therefore Doc has to remain a solo act in lieu of his mission, because some useless male idiot is just going to get in the way.

Nothing must stand in the way of Dr. Zeero Xiron convincing young women to masturbate to Satan. Fanatic worm wiggling to the Infernal Top Dog is an integral part of destroying the enslaving chains of Christianity. Why? Because it's a silly idea and not real, and it quickly makes the edifice crumble to ruin. Once you rub one out to The Devil, you never go back. Plus there is nothing hotter then a hyperventilating Pilgrim girl in the throes of a demonic sexual possession, just cranking one out to the Lord of the Black Sheep.

It is of crucial importance for Dr. Zeero to convince young women to masturbate to Satan – just as fanciful as the air we breathe, the H20 we slug & the fires that we kindle. It is the most vacant of to-do checkboxes beckoning for red ink...

Let us briefly examine the trials & tribulations of Magickal dating. There is the more normal playing field, then there is that of the Magickal Supervillain. Let us begin with the more normative dating circuit...

See, when dating other Magickal people, there is a great deal to consider. First thing's first – if you attempt to get in a relationship with someone who doesn't practice Magick it is ultimately doomed to fail. You can beat around the bush as much as you want – you can drag your relationship out for years but there will come a day when it just ends at a loggerheads. You will require the next step in the spiritual journey and they simply will not follow. So nip that shit in the bud.

A single person in youth can often get some hot nights. Perhaps you can sleep around with people not involved in Magick and maybe it's not a big deal for you. But when you actually start a relationship – it's not going to click.

Always remember that Magick is infinite because everyone's path is their own and what works for them might not work for others. From that standpoint we have infinite combinations. You have to really examine what traditions they are involved in and why? Ask yourself how comfortable you are in merging these things.

The Witch & The Magician – do they truly gel? If someone is hardcore Witch and not touching any of the Ceremonial Magick stuff, or vice versa, can you bridge that divide? Well you sure can through Cosmic Witchcraft.

All Witches are Pagans in that they are ultimately worshipping nature, but not all are Pantheists. Some are Monotheist like me. So you have to be very aware if your partner thinks the Gods & Goddesses & Daemons are real – as if people on an invisible plane who speak to them. Is this person delulu? Are they being "directed?" Are you "Pantheon Compatible?"

This is the slippery slope of Magick. Cranky ideas are one thing, but talking to invisible entities is a dangerous preoccupation. So you have to really know what they mean by *"the Gods and Goddesses call out to them,"* or the Infernal Divine. On that note, make sure to uncover if they are into Demonolatry.

Now the idea that you can truly date someone from one of the big religions... Well, does their scripture say to burn the Witches, kill or otherwise punish them? Can you honestly say that this is compatible or ignorable? If Jesus is in the picture you cannot get beyond that. Those other two big ones – one is a bit more compatible & friendly because they practice Magic. The other one – fat chance in hell.

All this Infernal Divine stuff – Doc would avoid crossing streams with any Left Hand Path folks. The women are expert seductresses and enchantingly charming, for sure. It is very hard to tell them "NO." But the men of the LHP? There is nothing more grotesque to me then the thought of bumpin' uglies with one of these gargoyles. Really, you think Black Magick Sorcerer archetype dude is hot? PUKE! *Cringe!* No sir-ree Bob. Nope nope nope.

Also, be mindful – if your partner is deep into Extreme Metal they are going to be obsessed with the dark aspects of Occultism and not much else. It's a narrow street. Many take all this Qliphotic trash dead serious yet have no clue what they are actually communicating. They are sentinels of Neanderthal Magick half-computed from half-read books by authors presenting scant references as Unholy Doctrine.

Secondly, if they have an upside down Pentagram they don't know shit about anything. This comes to us from a book Eliphas Levi wrote in the mid 1800's. No one in history ever used the upside down Pentagram. Levi invented it – and it meant that the elements controlled the Magician, that your head was in the dirt and you lost logic & reason for the animal senses and the instincts of the world. It meant you were out of control and your brain was made of mud. It meant you were a shitty Magician.

It wasn't until Anton Lavey appropriated the upside down Pentagram that anyone started to propagandize: *"It means you are your own God, bro."* That's just some hokey crap Lavey pulled out of his ass to rope everyone into the Church of Satan. Everywhere you turn these days – t-shirts & necklaces & tattoos – everyone just flashing ignorant bling.

These Extreme Metal types are obsessed with child's play, like the runes and all this Viking gibberish. Whooptie doo, we all get to go to Valhalla and butcher each other for all eternity! They don't stand for anything, just stabbing & hacking each other to pieces forever in the context of some partially recorded, mostly forgotten barbarian religion. Most Vikings were farmers anyway, and the ones who weren't were murderers, thieves and rapists.

Also, the most annoying subculture to date from is the Punk Rock crowd. Most of 'em are like, *"Leave your religion at the door, bro"* and throw Witchcraft in the same scrap pile. You talk about Magick or Ritual and they think you're talking about religion.

Furthermore, the point of Witchcraft force is that of manipulation. It doesn't mean a bad thing, it just means that you are transmuting on purpose. Good luck telling them that. They look at you as a sundry snake they have to kick out of their precious little underground. They think you are a devious con man and must be the Scene Police against you.

You cannot make the Punk crowd understand that they are utilizing Magick to project the world they want to see and that all of their concerts are rituals. Everything they are doing is some ritual to a Grand Notion that is essentially a Magickal Vision yet somehow not seen as such, because they simply cannot wrap their heads around it.

The Scene Police will come for you, with pitchforks & torches. You will never convince them that Magick is a part of Punk Rock, when Magick is the most Punk Rock thing in the entire world. I gave up even trying to communicate with them years ago, despite spending a lifetime among them. They do not find The Joke to be funny.

Also, if you can't get your Witchy boy/girlfriend out of a bar, can't get them out the house, can't get them to just directly go to nature & it's like dragging a horse to water – then you're with someone who looks the part and doesn't live it.

A lot of people are red herrings. A lot of goths look the part and pay lip service to Witchy stuff – many own Tarot decks or Magickal props. But if they are distanced from raw nature and don't care about it at all – just skip on it. Anytime you're introducing them to all kinds of material & concepts you cannot live without and it's like dragging a horse to water, it's time to get out of there.

Dating as a Magickal Supervillain is another paradigm entirely, and dating as a Queer Supervillain is even more mine-field laden. When you date another Supervillain this is much different than a Supervillain Team Up – fudge, this is when you feel anything at all. Supervillains are loners by nature and most have severe abandonment issues (among other psychological flaws). Most Supervillains totally reject any human touch or affection.

Still, Supervillains like to have hot sex every once in a while – and Sex Magick is of course a very important paradigm. But let's just call it – most Supervillains just downright can't stand other people. Antisocial obsessions reach zenith in Supervillainy. Still, as isolated as one becomes sometimes you still yearn for companionship…

First off, think hard of successful Supervillain relationships. The only one that ever seemed any good at navigating relationships in comic books was Harley Quinn because she hooked up with Poison Ivy. It's kind of amusing that the only working relationship in comics is lesbian in nature which is cool because A) Queer Power and B) they deserve each other. It's really good that she dumped The Joker anyway and we all wanted to see that because who the hell would want to date The Joker?

The relationship with Joker though – it represents so much of the conundrums in Supervillain dating. You don't just get treated as some distant Number 2 but you end up relegated as a henchman. You know how George Washington never quartered with his own soldiers because he had to keep that distance? You don't want to get buddy buddy with your Army. Sexuality is the same deal – never sleep with your henchman, henchwoman, non-binary goons, what have you.

Furthermore, it becomes a default S&M interplay when you get involved with your henchman because henchmen just love abuse. Trust me – making your henchman play Horsey is not as fun as it sounds. You waste all that bullwhip energy on flesh and not the humorless Superhero types you tussle with.

If you go full S&M do it with another Supervillain. The problem here is that most Supervillains are Doms – they want to dominate the world, they want to dominate the Superhero. It's a Dom thing most of the time, so their psychology won't allow them to submit to anything.

Now Doc here – if Xiron really likes someone enough, Doc will do anything. Doc spits blood for his loves. This is why anyone Doc ever dates, Doc just becomes their living Voodoo Doll. Xiron has a thing for absorbing other's trauma and taking it away – and there is nothing more romantic than clearing someone's head in this fashion.

Keep in mind most Supervillains have hair-trigger rejection policies, so if you say something really stupid it's going to be over in 2 seconds. Doc here has had a lot of trouble in this department because Xiron is a saucy, spicy, sarcastic motherf***er and has a tendency to say black humor things that don't always fly because it's not the 1990's anymore.

Keep in mind Doc is a Supervillain for the 90's – well I guess Anti-Hero if you choose it – but it's sort of like when Captain America was stuck in that block of ice for 20 years. They thawed him out and BAM – he was in the 60's. Same deal here – Doc is an anthropological curiosity hearkening back to 1996.

Ideological battles often result in devastation, so it's really important that you guys are really on the same platform. You need the same Zealot Mission because otherwise it's just going to go awry. Remember that nothing is going to make you want to hold someone's hand more than taking down the same Superhero or target.

Many Magickal Supervillains worship the figure of Satan or are literal Theistic Satanists. A Supervillain relationship can get annoying when they don't recognize you as Satan. You know, you can get jealous there. No matter how much you prove it, the proof just never stacks up to them. Satan proper is always going to take their heart before you get it in return. I guess you just got to ramp it up and make them understand your superiority.

Another problem – a lot of Supervillains are really into Azerate, right? And if you think you were jealous about Satan you have no idea how jealous you will become when ignored in lieu of the Shadow Of God. It's a giant Red Flag.

Another important dating tip is comparison of Magick techniques. It's very important your techniques key up on the same wavelength. Also, a comparison of aesthetic razzmatazz like, you know, your clothing styles and such – henchmen uniforms, complimentary masks. You don't want to be, like, wearing matching Nike tracks suits and going to the mall. Also difficult for Supervillains is that you have to set down your own Zealot Quest and actually aid your partner's Quest. "Sharing is Caring" – no matter how cringe it may be.

Back to the dating apps – let's talk Tinder. If you make a Tinder and list your name as " Supervillain" no one's going to touch you. So you have to lie – you can't post pictures with your Supervillain mask on or cape or whatever. But Tinder is a great way to lure people in and create more henchmen and Supervillains sometimes.

Also, it's quite romantic to carve, create & paint each other's masks. Or to present a mask to your Supervillain infatuation on Valentine's Day. Also, if you really want to bowl over your Supervillain date then bring them dead withered flowers – that always works right and, uh, give them a Whoopee Cushion too.

It's pretty romantic when you spring them from jail or from Arkham. Sometimes it's helpful when Supervillains are on the same mutual psych meds because it's a healthy relationship when you're on that plane together kind of reminding each other to take pills at the same time, right?

Another important item is Psychedelic Unison – that's the ultimate test. If they can eat fungus and be on that same level with you and all the walls are breathing & all the grass is moving – if they can hang they can last, right?

Also, how do they feel about homeless people? Bad taste is saying mean things about homeless people. A True Supervillain is down to help the homeless because a True Supervillain has probably been homeless many times because they're so busy concentrating on their Supervillain Masterplan that they can't reasonably work or hold an apartment. They're just so consumed by their villainous plot that everything else just gets in the way.

Be wary of their opinion of the Holy Guardian Angel. Also important to understand is their attitude towards The Golden Dawn. Furthermore, do they distrust Druids? Are they down with Druid rituals for the Pagan Community at large or do they just want to hijack it?

Lastly, you gotta ask is this Supervillain you're interested in – are they a Hellcat into Lilith? Cause this is going to tell you everything about a person. You must recognize that Lilith is going to take precedence over you and your relationship to them all the time. Backseat you go, Lilith in shotgun.

Ask yourself what you really seek in a relationship – do you want a henchman to push around, or do you want a date an equal?

Supervillains are megalomaniacs with egos the size of Jupiter but Supervillains also have this thing for which there is no term – their world domination libido. This merges with the sense of ego that the Magickal Body encapsulates.

Most people only think with ego & libido. They're not Magickal people or Supervillains – this is foreign territory for them. But you know us Magick folks – our whole combined Aura / Astral Body / Etheric Body / Intellectual Body / Spiritual Subconscious / Soul Contraption has a life of its own and combines to form its own sense of ego, per se, which is like your own individualized egregore. Like a hyper-complex morphogenic field, you know – there's all kinds of subtle energies going on there, all kinds of layers. But it's all collected as one big ol' thing, and that thing has its own sense of ego which could be bruised.

The point is that when you bruise another Supervillains' titanic ego, the shite will hit the fan. Therefore dumping another Supervillain who is all about you – things will get ugly. It's hard for a Supervillain to find love and they don't let it go without a fight. If all else fails, chances are the fight becomes a permanent duel. What a mess post-romantic war is with Supervillains! Doc must warn ye – be careful what you wish for in the first place, and be vigilant what an ugly end result may entail.

The more glaring answer is to have a discussion about red flags. We are human after all and chances are if you're a Magickal Supervillain then you're likely one horny little devil. So as the kids say these days, sometimes it's best to just quote / unquote "Hit It and Quit It."

Some red flaggy items to consider – it's a pretty big buzz kill knowing that no matter how much you prove yourself your Magickal Partner will always ignore you in favor of their Patron God / Goddess or Patron Demons / Daemons. If they are Left Hand Path then always expect the cold shoulder in lieu of Lilith, Satan or Samael. Fudge, they'll ignore you for someone far down the ladder – like a like a Vine or a Valac.

Really guys, Left Hand Path dating is a difficult racket. If you are both Satanists, you will constantly be trying to "out hardcore" each other dueling on who is more Satanic. Now it can be a healthy competition, but trust me, it usually turns to poop.

Pagan dating of Classic Witchcraft mindset is a much easier scenario. Keep in mind there are plenty of old school Witches definitely rocking the Supervillain aesthetic – you just gotta key them into what they're doing. Sometimes they don't think of themselves like that and sometimes they're very open to it.

Realize any Magickal person can be a Supervillain – we got the Supervillain Druids, Heathens, Picts, Chaos Magicians, Ninjas. The sky is the limit! Hell, we got Supervillain Shamans & Alchemists and all kinds of Occultists.

But understand, there will likely also come a time when you may need to dump your Supervillain partner. Well dummy you asked for it and then you got it and then you didn't want it anymore. If you made their shriveled Grinchy heart pump just a little and you smash that glimmer of hope, I guess you understand what it's like to be a fly in the spider's web, just waitin' for that spider to come up n' eat ya.

The truth is that there is no easy way to do it – you just find a way and run for cover. Cobra Commander said it best: *"Cobra Retreat!"* You're ex will instantly be rendered a Serpentor so, uh, you know, your head is going on their mantle. Unless you dump them for a far stronger, more dynamic, more deadlier Supervillain cause, let's face it – once you go Ultimate Adversary you never go back. Point is, date a killer Heel and don't waste your time with a Jobber. Any other line of thinking is purely kayfabe.

Also a few random things – a lot of Supervillains like Black Metal. Pay close attention to what they are jamming cause you don't want that Left Hand saluting The Right Wing if you catch my drift. It's a real problem out there.

Also, most Supervillains find GG Allin pretty hilarious, but the question is do they really know about him and to what extent of his antics are they really down with? Furthermore, quickly find out if they are into Black Sabbath. If they don't dig Tony Iommi guitar solos they aren't worth a one night stand. Also never bang someone who likes Five Finger Death Punch, it means they are a big old Oscar Meyer wiener mobile with flat tires...

This next subject is sure to roil some feathers, but hopefully the feathers of Malek Taus. People got urban chicken farms, but where's all the peacocks, eh? Anyway, we now turn our attention to the Queer scene and LGBTQ+ dating.

Again, recognize the intelligence writing these words. As a pansexual I could go in any direction – however there are still all kinds of people who make me barf in my mouth. Just because I technically could be sexual with any gender doesn't mean I actually want to. 99% of the time my mind will be on a subject other then sexual gratification. Most people I don't even notice. They are stagnant & boring as a piece of furniture.

Nothing is more revolting then an older man calling himself "daddy" and a young guy playing the role of "boy." The fact that this is such a part of gay culture means that a huge portion of gay culture must also be destroyed with the nuclear attack precision that is reserved for both MAGA and the Abrahamic Monotheist travesty.

Understand that when you identify yourself as a Queer Supervillain you are kind of "othering" yourself. It's important to just think of yourself as "A" Supervillain. This is not to hide who you are, don't get me wrong. I'm just saying it helps to focus. If you wanna be loud & proud about it, that's all your choice and that's absolutely fine.

Think in terms of this – being queer is who you are. It doesn't have to define your personality or way you dress or interact or body movements – it's just something that is. You don't have to put rainbows & pink triangles on your Supervillain costume. You don't gotta wear it on your sleeve. You don't need gadgets shaped like phallus – none of that goofy shit. Save that for *Orgazmo* – let Ron Jeremy have 'em. You absolutely do not need to play into any of these stereotypes. Your Supervillain path is not a straight white male comedy starring Ben Stiller & Vince Vaughn.

Now the problem here – it's all about stereotypes. If you openly tell people "*I am a Gay Supervillain*," the sheer menace of your diabolical scheme is somehow gonna be seen as a little less sinister. Well at first, right? Basically you have this handicap where you really gotta prove yourself and show them the level of Satan that you actually are.

The big hang up is this gibberish where people hear that you are gay and what pops in their ignorant cis-heteronormative minds is that you must be wearing a hot pink cape – I mean hotter pink then Bret Hart's spandex tights – and that you probably act like some queeny, draggy, twinky, ultra effeminate guy. As if you must speak with a corny forced lisp and flop around flaming with girly limp wrists.

Like I said – you really have to step up. Make these people realize that you mean business. You are the League of Shadows and you are here to fulfill Ra's Al Ghul's destiny. You were born in the darkness, molded by it. The shadows betray them, because they belong to You. It's important to intellectually rationalize these things.

Speaking of cis-hetero people... It's almost 2025. Queer people have existed since the dawn of time yet barely our world has come to acceptance. In many parts of the world they will execute you, imprison you, punish or torture you. And if you think queers aren't persecuted enough already, you have no idea the court persecutions against openly queer, openly Supervillains. In some countries they will bury you to your head in sand and stone you to death just for being gay. But a Supervillain too? *Hot damn!*

I mean us Supervillains – we are the minority, man. And if you feel persecuted because you're queer to begin with, you have no idea how much you will be persecuted as a Queer Supervillain. So we provoke insane tortures here.

That's why America – despite all its problems & being a Chumptatorship – it's still a Magickal Wonderland for Queer Supervillains because its not illegal to be gay (*currently*) or a Supervillain (*for now*). But I guess we'll have to see about that one now, won't we?

In 2025, LGBTQ+ are much more tolerated. However, that cis-hetero straight world – what do they really think? What do they tell themselves quietly in their own minds or mutter underneath their breath?

What I'm getting at is to use their homophobia against them. Making straight people uncomfortable by your sexuality and what you represent is like wielding a Magickal forcefield that can manipulate anyone easily. It is an art form; it is literally a branch of Magick. You can use peoples own homophobia against them like a puppet master.

Furthermore, never underestimate Grindr as a weapon of war. As a gay male Supervillain, you have the henchmen advantage. If you are even reasonably attractive then endless idiot men will send tsunamis of NSFW pics with that trouser snake flashing.

Use these buffoons like an endless reservoir. Make them drive you around. Make 'em buy you things – use 'em for all their worth. Then sacrifice your pawn. You don't gotta give 'em no play. You don't owe 'em shit – just blue balls everywhere, jazzed up in perpetual torment. You know, like two Pluto's beneath the belt? Boo hoo hoo, poor men.

I guess it would be fair at this point to mention Lesbian Supervillain aesthetic... The truth is that you women, you got your shit figured out. You don't need me mansplaining nothing to you. I'm so proud of you all, you are so wonderful. Men are useless and you are so lucky you have zero attraction to them. You win the lottery of genetics.

Anyway, one drawback – it is wildly unpopular in the gay male community to openly declare yourself a Supervillain. They're not gonna get The Joke. So be prepared to find yourself alienated & exiled into a corner of the queer bar at your own table. Because all those college educated, middle class professionals – they're not gonna speak a word to you, no matter how hot you are. And all that's left are like creepy S&M kink guys who no one wants to screw anyway because they are grotesque.

If that's your bag then go for it – but Doc would warn against being "Pup Handled" because that isn't very Supervillain-like. But hey, just cause it sinks my boat doesn't mean it won't float yours.

Also, a great way to make Gay Supervillain henchmen is by being a Bathhouse Marauder. It's easy – you just walk around in a towel for a few hours and the next thing you know you got 50 cell numbers of useless men to just drive your ass around the city organizing your next Supervillain assault & getting your masterplan in order...

So, back to Black Magick Momma. I encountered her at the crack park – she was waiting on the gazebo, trying to be spooky & mysterious. She was looking to invade Portland and get a Coven going. I was very direct – I'd just broken up with this girl I was crazy about all year, and I was a sad sack, disoriented mess.

She was immediately interested in the girls I hung out with all Summer – who had actually ditched me to hook up as a lesbian couple. All year I exposed them to witchy books & concepts. They were a prime target for this invading Magickal Dictator and all her wily plans. I wasn't a dummy – I knew the score.

This woman, with her bulletbelt & cloth headdress – she was a no-bullshit Black Metal vampire Witch lady. Short & curvy, her aura was "take no prisoners." She sensed the girls I just broke off from were ripe for a freshly minted Coven. And this woman – she was just like myself and both of those lezzie girls combined.

We went out to the goth club, drank a bit. She tried to take me home. I was so disheveled & heartbroken I just let her go alone so I could continue wallowing in depression. I had asked The Gods to being me my Life Partner, this chick shows up and now I was simply walking away? Throwing in the towel because the lingering influence of some Normy pushing Kabbalah?

I woke up the next day and realized what I had done. I thought it was through and felt like such an asshole. I lunged for the phone & left a message. After a few hours of nervous pacing the phone rang. She agreed to meet again.

I went over to her place. She was staying with a cousin and had brought her altar in a luggage case along with some of her most prized books. Things I never saw again anywhere else, as deep into Magick as I became – manuals on all this Lilithian / Luciferian psychic vampirism stuff, all this Qliphotic crap that these Black Metal bands were always referencing but just seemed like unappealing gibberish to me. I was so blind back then it was pitiful. I was ignorantly promoting this bullshit the entire time as a metal journalist because it was all garbled nonsense to me.

She left the room and I touched her evil plant. And when she came back in she shouted: "*Don't touch it!*" I lied & pretended to never have. Then she decided to make me her Magick slave. She washed me in the shower in all 4 directions and anointed me with all kinds of oil, washing me ritualistically. Black Magick Momma, I am a junkie for your demons. Let me receive them all!

I was more interested in The Game then I was her – I wanted to ingest all her dark clouds and mess with the ritual. I kept standing in all the wrong directions on purpose, disrupting her operation. I screwed it up on purpose, pretending I was ignorant. Another goal post passed!

We attempted to have sex that night, but it was the first time my junk never worked! Try as I may, that elephant trunk was limp as a wet noodle. Her Magickal Aura was so frigid, icy and Necrodaimonic it shriveled my raisins!

I apologized profusely, and we soon fell asleep. She was out cold and I was awake alone. I felt like a total loser. Outside her door, in the still house, I could hear hooves stomping around the living room. It literally felt & sounded like there was a creature of darkness lurking beyond the door.

We parted and all I could think of was The Game. I felt nothing for her. My entire aura rejected her. I couldn't wait to see her again.

For whatever reason, our communications broke down. She tried to meet with the girls but I couldn't get them in one place. And Black Magick Momma had to let it happen naturally – she had to work her mystique. That's the whole theatrical game of Witchcraft and I was messing up her whole approach. Well no shit, I was doing so on purpose. She thought she'd anointed me her slave, but she was another pawn in my grip. She had no idea who she was really dealing with.

I was still infatuated with the Normy. We were talking again and I thought it was going to happen. I had to make a choice on a Friday night – go for the one I really wanted to be with? Or straight into Vampire Lady Dominatrix land? I had an option of either – but I left the Witch in the dust to stumble after hopeless hopes of the Normy.

Normy picked me up – it was the moment I looked in the mirror and said to myself, *"finally, you could just be like everyone else."* She had Magic Mushrooms but I was hesitant. We went to the nightclub and danced to some techno. Right when I thought we were going to hook back up she realized what I was thinking and contracted. Said we had to split.

She abruptly drove me home and just kind of dumped me off there. She would have just ditched me there regardless, all insane on mushrooms. It was so low. I felt very dejected and amazed she would be that careless to my psychology. Don't just twist someone's mind on psychedelic drugs and abandon them at peak. No clue, no empathy.

After awhile, the Witch gave up on Portland and went back to her home state. We had a final text exchange where she was telling me to screw myself and I was glorifying her with every response. She wanted me to make some grand "don't go" sort of plea and just wasn't getting it from me. I just kept telling her that she woke me up and I kept thanking her. I didn't care what The Gods had decided – you ain't for me, lollipops...

Over the next few months I felt like that tree I touched was slowly draining me. Was I going mad? I felt that only Magick could defeat this freakish conundrum. I started my research once again, long since ignored. I began with Buckland's *Scottish Witchcraft*.

This leads me to studying my Scottish Ancestors, The Picts who were named such after "pictures" because they were covered in tattoos. They wore steel dog collars & walked around naked all the time, having constant orgies. They were fierce maniac warriors rubbing psychedelic mushroom batter all over their bodies before combat. I was totally of their ilk...

Learned more about my heritage, The Druids – all this Pagan Celtic stuff. The psychic poison? Getting worse & worse. I was living at a house where music was supposed to be the point, but I had quit playing music for a year. All this activity was in the basement – concerts raging, bands practicing, albums recording – yet I kept hiding in my room researching Dark Paganism.

My roommates didn't understand what I was up to, or where I was heading. They weren't really down with this Witchcraft stuff because they didn't take it serious. To them it was all "woo woo" trash about Astrology & Crystals & Palm Reading. They had no frame of reference for anything I was espousing.

My fortunes lifted thanks to OkCupid. In my forlorn funk I began talking to some random person as you always do on dating platforms. Soon she came over – she was Black & Jewish. She dressed low-key – just kind of blended in and wasn't showy whatsoever. She dressed like a 1980's elementary school teacher. She had these thick nerdy glasses, and if you just pulled them off like in some corny Disney movie she immediately blossomed.

We weren't very connective in terms of dialogue, but me oh my, she was quite a hellcat in the physicality department. She was heavily sexual. I tried to have lengthy discussions but she just kind of seemed bored or annoyed. She wanted physical touch & intimacy – everything else took a back seat.

We got along well enough but I never really knew how to click with her. I gradually stopped responding to her. In my head I didn't think she was all that into me and it was an awkward fling. Apparently she was crazy about me and I had no idea. When I backed off she stopped talking because self esteem issues. Either way she vanished and would turn up a little later in this tale. I apparently broke her heart and had no clue.

As spring led into summer I began getting messages about my mother having a Chairi Malformation. I was getting calls and asked if I had seen weird behavior – missing time, blacking out. It was like a pinprick of light that started the total recall.

Again long story, but I'll put it like this – I grew up a loner only child with a single mother who wasn't "all there." She was quite a piece of work, let me tell you. Her brain problem worked on her as if a tumor and she was scrambled. I tried to tell the outside world but no one would do anything or listen.

I was forced to normalize all kinds of weird behavior & ideas & viewpoints & communication. Furthermore, she was kind of a simpleton in many ways (just like Doc Zeero) – and she was a hardcore Irish Catholic Bible Thumper constantly quoting the most violent & barbaric aspects of scripture. "Eye for An Eye" was her favorite part of The Bible. Of all the ideas available she clung to that the most.

She was also the most homophobic person I ever met in my entire life. So creepy and violent were her views that even if I presented them to you, dear reader, you would never believe such a person could exist. She was like one of those Westboro Baptist Church people, with their "God Hates Fags" signs and shriveled hate filled faces shouting their contempt.

She was hardcore MAGA long before MAGA existed, as well as my Stepfather. She was a secretary for the Police, and he was a cop and Vietnam Veteran. As you can suspect they were not a joy to live under the watchful eye of. It is amazing the finesse by with I learned to dodge these people as a young person.

When I was 18 I finally escaped her constant threats of boot camp or mental hospitalization. She was like a weasel who stalked me trying to micromanage every aspect of my life. She was the craziest person I ever met who was assured the she was the sanest one on the face of the planet. She was a master manipulator and textbook narcissist with defeatist, hopeless views towards so many aspects of life and existence. All she did was bitch.

The story was complicated though, and much of my life was fuzzy to me. There were huge blocks of time I couldn't quite remember, as I turned manic depressive and schizoid by age 13. Untreated, I kept it all to myself. These were some dark, freakish years full of flights of fantasy to escape the turgid reality I was entrapped by.

Memories were jagged and restarted at a certain point. I was about 10, and then I was about 12. From age 13 onward, it became clearer. Basically I had my first schizophrenic bout in 8th grade, Fall 1994 to Spring 1995. I could always remember from thereon out. Anything before was scattered.

Anyway, it was now May 2016. I woke up and suddenly remembered what I was blacking out and running from the whole time. Everything was a sick dream in another dream in another. I had been boxed in and I needed to fight my way out...

To explain what is going on here would take 100 pages, and I still don't think you'd ever believe me. Furthermore, it's a dark personal tale that I don't feel comfortable broadcasting to the whole world. Avoiding it will prevent me from making complete sense, so therefore I must remark something.

To put it most basic – in January 1992, on a snowy dark Saturday, my mom's tumor-like problem "took the wheel." I quickly realized how scary of a person I was really locked in isolation with. A very strange and dark scene unfurled.

It was the end of my childhood, instantly. I turned to my schoolteachers – I tried to get the authorities to intervene but it failed. They did not listen nor did I even understand how to properly communicate what had happened. All I could do was withdraw and stammer.

They sent me back home with her, and she was extremely pissed and terrifying. From thereon I became a literal prisoner of sorts, micromanaged and harassed by someone missing marbles in a very bad way. I slowly drifted away into my own reality inside my own mind. Over time, I blacked out the dark scene. Everything I once was was now trapped there – and in response I became more of an idea then a person.

Again, long story, but the day she went over the edge she had gone to the plant nursery. She came back looking like she was high – like she huffed something that triggered her and sent her over the edge. It just seemed like there was some extra component to this mess. I went to that same nursery and searched high and low for something, anything, which also might impact me the same. Maybe there was an answer. But as things grew worse, I quickly forgot this pursuit as if a distant echo.

When I came to at the age of 35, I remembered that particular day – and very soon I remembered that tree. I wondered if that thing I touched The Witch owned was somehow connected. I began looking into the history of my family and our crest from Scotland – it was oak, a Druid thing. Maybe something connected to our lineage and environment historically was the answer? Perhaps The Druids would know – they worshipped trees, after all. They had a number of scared trees. What was the missing connection?

I met Jess at Drum & Bass night. She was a lanky, full figured woman with green hair. Alone in the corner having a nervous breakdown, I thought she was quite attractive. I didn't know her name – I just kind of waved and she waved back, but was clearly in her own world and not looking for company.

I woke up the next day and in the brisk morning air I looked to the hill in the distance with all the rich homes atop it. I felt The Universe tap me on the shoulder and say: *"What is it that you desire? Anything – it's yours."* I said to that inner voice: *"That woman to be my partner and to live in one of those big houses up there."*

The next week I went back to the club and got her number. That Friday – Beltaine weekend – she picks me up at night. Takes me on a drive to the deep country to the deep woods telling me all about how a Black Magick Witchcraft Coven is stalking her, and that we have to unite to end their games.

And how her ex boyfriend she was all devastated from – he was originally from my home state and he was a creepy Black Magick Occult guy in the Rave Scene. And I remembered his name and that he was my unknown adversary back when I used to throw rave parties. Never met him though. He was aggressively uniting all the creepy Black Magick females he could find in the rave scene.

So this girl, obsessed with *Twin Peaks*, drives me to this secret grove that looks like it's where Druids would have Mistletoe rituals. Tells me all about the Dark Coven stalking her. Then she just jumps on me and we go at it like rabbits, swearing an oath to take down the cult in our midst.

Next morning we wake in the car – takes me to a fake Stonehenge structure someone created in the wilderness. We make out on this Druid structure as if part of a ritual and she drives me back. Again, I was more interested in The Game then the girl. All she did was whine about her lame ex boyfriend anyway. I didn't really care about her, just like Black Magick Momma. I wanted to play Magick and this was an excuse.

The next day Jess picks me up and drives me right to the top of the hill I looked to fatefully a week prior. Takes me right to the coolest looking house up there and parks outside. Tells me: *"I want to be your girlfriend and I want one of these houses and to live there as soon as we can and constantly have S&M rave parties and then every night I want you to BLEEEEEEEEEP."*

So we drive away, go to her house. I got the info on all members of the Dark Coven stalking her – all their faces, all their names. Jess left. While alone I performed a Binding Spell – classic witchy, just like old times. I called to anything & everything that was attached to me from past actions – ghosts, spirits, demons, Gods, Daemons – these women want you. They want your baggage. Go to them, I command you. Free me.

Even though it was in my head, I felt every last dark cloud leave me. And I was alone again in a big empty house, and I walked outside. Clear blue sky. No ghosts, no baggage – just me. They get whatever was coming to 'em. Soon after, I dumped Jess by text message and ghosted her completely. She was in the way of The Game.

Shortly afterwards I had a breakthrough on the plant. I found this lecturer on social media doing a video series on The Sacred Yew. He was calling himself a Yew Shaman. He was traveling the world going to ancient Yews and just communing with them & huffing their potent Taxine – having all kinds of esoteric experiences.

Then I found a video of a guy saying a bulb grew on top of the tree every thousand or so years, but it was a big secret. That sounded to me like the Druid Mistletoe Ritual. What was this? I started digging in. When I looked back to find this video, it had vanished completely. But it gave my mind a wild way to approach The Yew.

I returned to work, the gay bar. More harassment from the asshole bartender & shit talker usuals. Nearly Asexual, hates gay culture – I was a pariah backed in a corner, and I was the one who wanted to live the gay lifestyle more then any of them. I was the desperate one clinging to hope of a life which effortlessly came to them.

They couldn't bang me so they had to lie and turn me into a psycho creep. Dirty protester, Heavy Metal scoundrel. All of them & their Heckle & Jeckle acts. And now here I was talking about this weird tree, totally embroiled in it. They could not see the brilliance.

All of this Celtic Pagan research I was doing that was returning me to my Magickal path intersected into looking hard at this mysterious plant that I soon learned all kinds of fantastic details about. And as my research continued, it kept finding it hooked more & more into Magick.

As a Witch learning all of this, the Tree became a Pagan idol of worship. The Viking World Tree Yggdrasil was before me and huff on its hallucinogenic gasses I did. I went to the plant nursery and acquired a specimen – it was like a puppy that just leaped into my arms. These are outdoor plants but I of course kept it in my room. After 12 hours of typing I went outside – I was high on its fumes. The world was Magickal. The colors bright, like absinthe. My psychic senses were flared. I felt like a black cat in the night.

The Tree directed me – kept showing me things & what to Google. By July 2016 I was 100% plant. I had released my books as a publishing company and was set to release my magnum opus memoir on Halloween – I should have been pushing that. Instead I joined someone's band and began planning a European tour. Should have been focused on that too. But The Tree had me – this device to explore all Magick. I had no choice but to combine all the data into a massive Info Comp.

My friend from high school who also lived in Portland died in 2015. When we were in our early 20's, we got really into Black Metal. Like a high school research project, he had a binder of material he printed out from the internet. He was charting all these Pagan references in this Black Metal music. He got very far but it was ultimately incomplete. He had turned away from the music and dive-bombed into heroin. It took many years but that's what finally did him in.

He was gone and now I would finish his research – The Yew was now the direction it would supplant. Little did I know it was turning into a 666 page monster for Samhain – to end up as an 888 page beast on Yule.

Again, like a flash, another budding relationship appeared. I had met these two women – both sex workers – who were inseparable. One of them took a fancy to me and came over. Tiny & tatted with a black humor obsession and a perversity I could not even fathom, she was everything I once sought after until this recent Magickal change. Once I would have killed for her as a young man but I had changed fanatically. I found her black humor in bad taste.

We ended up getting close, you know, and when she took off her pants I was thinking *"That's it, I can finally be like everyone else. This is–"* then I saw the gigantic tattoo of Lilith on her inner thigh, and my junk shriveled up like a prune.

Magick now had taken my life by storm to the point where the concept of Magickal Hygiene was right in my face. *I would be a sell out if I had sex with this scorching hot woman!* She was a member of the worst cult on Earth and most dangerous faction of Black Magick that has ever existed. I could have no part of it! *What had I become?!?*

I went through the motions of making out, but we didn't actually have sex. She wasn't feeling it that day – *luckily*. I don't know what I would have said or done had she made a move and I had to reject her for this reason. What would I say? *"Sorry Toots, you're part of an evil cult so take a hike?"* And what then – I'd have an army of dyed red hair Lilith Witches stalking me because I broke their Infernal Sister's heart?

I hung out with this girl one more time, but I intentionally did not wear my Sunday's best. I looked like a slob and put zero effort into making her interested. I presented myself as scattered and uninteresting. I basically went on an anti-date to convince her to look the other way. It worked – I had successfully deflected my Dream Girl! After all, she was only in the way of The Tree...

The more I hung out with the European Yew, the more the psychic poisoning of the Suicide Forest wore off. Even if it was entirely in my own mind, the counterbalance saved me. Placebo or not, it did it's job – Yggdrasil saved me from the clutches of the Lilithian Qliphotic Vampire.

So why The Yew? Understand all this was a slow incremental process to learn, but I'm just going to dump all this on you now. To be honest, 2016 isn't all that exciting – mostly staring at a computer & huffing Yew fumes.

Let's just imagine you're at a bus stop, just waiting & waiting. It's night time, a perfect 70 degrees. No matter how long you wait, the bus never comes. This random guy walks up from the shadows, oddly lucid & hyped. He asks if you're bored, and you say *"yes,"* because that next bus is dragging hard. So the mystery man starts ranting about this weird tree. And it sounds strange at first, but he ropes you in.

He's possessed by wild enthusiasm over some "Life Tree" that connects everyone, everything, all religions. And you get so into the story that once the bus shows up, you don't want to go home, you just stand there, waving the bus on for the next ride, because now you have to know everything this guy is jabbering about.

So think of this next barrage as that wild kind of street corner chat. And by the time we're done here, you will thank me. See, The Yew releases a hallucinogenic gas called Taxine that creates a disassociative trance widely connected with shamanism & psychic phenomena – including telepathy, telekinesis & Astral Projection.

For over 450k years of human development we've been psychically & physically accustomed in a positive way to the stimulation of this plant in our natural environment. Therefore, "sensing" this low-level alkaloid in minor capacity is not a longing addiction for a drug, but is akin to sensing a presence.

The Yew has a property which makes a human "sense the presence" of living fauna in a way that other plants do not. There is something that connects us deeply to The Yew Tree, and it is reputed to restore health, both physically & psychically. Which is exactly why The Druids & Celtic Pagans worshipped this thing – the older the tree, the more intense the potency & effect.

Mythology or not, the commonly occurring link between all recorded psychic phenomenon – be it telepathy, telekinesis, levitation, "poltergeist" activity, "Witchcraft manifestation" – has to do with disassociation.

Total disassociation is always the intent of deep meditation. In Wicca/Witchcraft, Witches gather to meditate with one another to create a mutual human circle of disassociation. Together they form an intended link – a concentration based upon both dropping out of reality by merging with the universal unconsciousness & physical world at once. "One-ness" is the key, all while meditating upon outcome, intention or desire.

Witchcraft Covens are in this sense psychically linked disassociation as an attempt to manifest reality, in total harmonization of mind & spirit with the physical realm, both seen & unseen – or simply to channel the forces of nature. Whether or not "energy" can actually physically or psychically be manipulated through these actions, the main concern is meditative self-control to harness energies & manifest realities.

Thus, the importance of The Yew in Paganism is profound – and absolutely crucial to our understanding of Celtic Witchcraft, Germanic Paganism & The Druids.

Taxine somehow affects the part of the brain that differentiates full consciousness and, say, "sleepwalking," "hypnosis," or "deep meditation" at varying degrees, all dependent upon the biological chemistry of the person in contact with it. Most have minor reactions, some have extremely positive ones; others have uneasy or harsh feelings. Some, it seems, totally trigger into something latent & untapped.

It appears everywhere in legend & lore, in artifacts & archaeology – yet it's consistently assumed as merely a symbol. Everyone knows "The Tree Of Life" – yet the integral history has been largely forgotten and intentionally buried. Its history is not just with these "ancient sorcerers" & "godless heathens" – The Yew impacts all of the major world religions – and especially Judaism & Christianity.

The travesty here is that the Ancient Roman Empire, under the command of Julius Caesar, aggressively wiped out The Druids & their practices surrounding this tree. Once the Empire outlawed Paganism, anyone caught performing rituals with this tree was put to death. The Church was highly integral in weaning the population from The Yew & any remainder of its ancient meanings.

A massive key to our forgotten past – most of what is now the UK, as well as huge swathes of France, Belgium, Netherlands & Germany were a massive Ancient Yew forest. Almost all of Scotland, England, Ireland & Wales was once what is now famously known as the "Japanese Suicide Forest" – the haunted forest of Mt. Fuji known for giving people "bad trips" and unstable mental conditions.

The difference is the strain – the Taxus Baccata Yew covered Celtic Europe. The Japanese Strain (as well as the strain populating the Middle East & Asia), is known for it's more unstable conditions.

It seems that these "Druids" which populated the British Isles – what a "field day" it must have been for these "wise men" to preside over a vast Yew Grove & its denizens (who were already worshiping the plant) eager to be guided?

The Ancient Celtic burial grounds were covered in Yew Trees. They'd bury corpses and plant Yews on top. The ancient Pagans literally thought the tree absorbed the soul, and their ancestors lived on through the life-force of the tree, because the tree was psychically connected to humanity.

It sure seems that during Samhain The Druids were getting high as a kite off this Hallucinogenic Yew Gas on Halloween and were using their freaky trances to ritualistically "talk to the dead."

The Druids & Celts of Europe were in close continual contact with ancient Yew groves – specimens existing perhaps hundreds of thousands of years. We cannot grasp the mind of the Ancient Celts because they were absorbing Taxine in quantities we cannot fathom; the older the tree, the more potent the effect.

At phenomenally higher qualities we'd been exposed to it constantly through our developmental stages as a vast human organism. In the mother's womb the child absorbs the mood swings and psychic phenomena which even sensing the Taxine stimulates and the embryonic brain develops in response. It's not crazy talk – we are connected to this thing in a way we don't understand; even the trees growth mimics the embryology of a developing fetus in many ways.

Unlike today, The Yew was plentiful throughout Europe & The British Isles. There were specimens possibly 100,000+ years old, and immense Yew forests covered huge swathes of territory. Scotland was once like a deep Amazon of Yew.

In many aspects the tree mimics a vegetative form of a human embryonic process as it grows. The tree bleeds; it hollows itself like a developing skull.

The Yew is planted all over sacred Pagan burial grounds; most churches simply built over them, with extreme care in making sure it's roots went through graves. In life, these people felt spiritually in tune with this tree – they were a part of it, literally connected to it. Thus, it seems the belief was the souls of the dead would through nature be absorbed into the life-force of the tree, would be coalesced like primal memory.

The Yew is known as "The Witches Tree." Practitioners of Witchcraft or Wicca (or nature absorption Ch'I) felt they could connect with their ancestors through The Yew, that "Witches of Old" were be born again in the life-force of The Tree.

ANU/DANU/DANA, the Irish Mother Witch & Goddess of the Underworld (Witch Goddess of The Yew's root world) – was its symbolic figure. In the German/Norse lands, the Witches of Fate lived in the trunk of the tree, guiding past, present and future. They were the 3 Witches of Wyrd, the Nornir's.

The Picts were inhabiting these immense and ancient groves of Yews since the dawn of time. While I can find no direct proof to validate my claim that the Picts were using The Yew as a Magickal centerpiece – it is absurd to think they would somehow never have caught on. They lived in an endless forest of ancient Yew. All of Scotland was once, as we modernly deem it, a Japanese Suicide Forest.

These trees were destroyed en masse for war materials and intentional destruction campaigns – plus Catholic insistence to hack them down as the newly invented "Christmas Tree."

Splicing The Yew's meditative abilities with "Elemental Vampirism" represents something very potent for the Occult/Wiccan/Pagan community. A less negative sounding term for this is what a Taoist might call "Tree Cycling." Elemental Vampirism is the total opposite of draining a living being for exploitation – it is the practice of drawing Mana from the physical universe.

Yew Tree // Taxus Baccata // Cultivar: Fastigiata (Druids) & Fastigiata/Stricta (Modern); Witches Tree, Tree of Resurrection, Tree of Eternity, "Tree Of Life." In the early life of flora, The Yew was probably the only evergreen tree in Britain.

The Yew is the only living creature biologically capable of living indefinitely; when not tampered with, they are essentially immortal. They can literally resurrect themselves as long as the smallest amount of root remains connecting soil & Tree. Because of its ability to produce new shoots almost anywhere, it is able to quickly heal.

In some aspects, The Yew's growth mimics the embryology of a developing human fetus. The Yew expands both upwards & downwards at once, as if a mirror reflection. It sends its energy to the tops of the branches which reach back down into the earth to act again as roots, The Tree cloning itself indefinitely & creating waves of "Yew Tunnels."

The Yew is a loner and generally grows isolated. So long as the trunk of the tree is 6 ½ inches or more in height, it will regenerate. The Yew hollows out as time passes, leaving no tree rings to determine its age. This gives it flexibility in windy conditions.

They grow within themselves with a new trunk from the husk of old, with new shoots from the base. As these develop they coalesce with the main trunk, appearing as 'fluting', or ridges becoming thick enough to support the tree. When the original trunk decays this secondary growth forms the new tree. While the center is rotting a branch may put down a root into the decaying material, so that in decay new life is provided.

When a branch reaches the ground it can become embedded in the soil – The Yew Tunnel. From this point a new tree can develop, either joined to the parent or living separately. Likewise a root close to the ground may give rise to new growth at some distance from the parent.

The oldest Yews have often become two or more 'fragment' trees. These may still be connected to the origin below ground, or each may exist in its own right as a separate tree – doubling, tripling or even quadrupling the chances of survival.

Its thick canopy prevents moisture & rot. The dead wood that surrounds decaying heartwood – this lasts so long that new growth from the base is given centuries to establish itself. In this time the new or secondary growth is established.

Yew is widely recorded as "The Witches Tree" and has strong connotations to Wicca/Witchcraft, as well as many Pagan agriculture/fertility Goddesses. The Yew is sacred to Hecate and the Crone aspect of the Triple Goddess.

The Yew releases a hallucinogenic gas called Taxine; the male plant gives off more Taxine then the female plant. Release of Taxine is strong in summer heat, but even stronger in winter (Yule Time).

In Judaism the Tree of the Adam & Eve myth was a Yew. The Kabbalistic Tree Of Life is a Yew. The tree Buddha gained his enlightenment from was (likely) in The Yew family. The Viking Life Tree Yggdrasil was a Yew & the source of Odin's enlightenment. Asgard is located in Yew Valley, surrounded by The Yew River.

In Irish mythology, The Yew was The Tree Of Ross -- one of the 5 sacred trees brought from The Otherworld at the division of the land into 5 parts. It was said to be the 'offspring of the tree that is in Paradise." It was sacred to Banbha, the death-aspect of the once-supreme Triple Goddess. In Britain it was also associated with Hecate. Yew was one of the 9 sacred trees for kindling Beltane fires.

The bark produces a cancer slowing agent named Taxol. Yew was sometimes called "The Forbidden Tree" and used to stimulate abortions, while its poison was used in small amounts as a cardiac stimulant. The older specimens "bleed" a red substance that looks like human blood.

Yew = 5th vowel and last letter of the Druid Ogham alphabet – IDHO. Yew embodies "The Crone aspect of the Triple Goddess." Runes: YR / EIHWAZ / EOLH

The Fortingall Yew, a male plant at perhaps 9000 years old, recently changed the sex of one branch only and produced berries. Trees typically go male to female, sometime are hermaphroditic (as is The Yew), but this is an anomaly. They are thought to have descended from PALEOTAXUS REDIVIVA, found imprinted on a Triassic era fossils.

Fossils of Yew have been found from the Jurassic era. They grew in great abundance during the Ice Age. As the glaciers receded, the forests of Europe contained up to 80% Yew.

Symbolism: Immortality, Rebirth, Protection, Longevity, Change, Divinity, Strength, Power, Honor, Silence, Mystery, Illusion, Victory, Sanctity, Leadership, Introspection. Magickal Associations: Immortality, renewal, regeneration, rebirth, everlasting life, transformation, protection against evil, connecting with ancestors, shamanism, dreaming, heightening psychic abilities. Yew is used in spells to raise the spirits of the dead or contact Daemons.

It was known in Europe as "The Death Tree" because its bark, foliage & fruit are all poisonous. Every part of The Yew is poisonous to digest except for the fleshy part of the berry (*used as a diuretic or laxative*). The seed inside the berry is deadly if it cracks open while chewing or ruptures during digestion. The leaves are more toxic than the seed.

However, the tree is not toxic to the touch. Fatal poisoning in humans is very rare – occurring with 50 to 100 grams of leaves or chewing on the bark. Even the dust from sanding is poisonous. Dog poisoning usually happens playing "fetch" with a Yew stick. Canine's naturally avoid evergreen conifers by scent, although a puppy or kitten might nibble on the leaves if kept indoors.

The word Yew comes from the Anglo-Saxon "Giuli" which is the stem for "Yule." The Yule Log was originally a piece of Yew. Set on the hearth, it burned for 12 days over the midwinter season.

Both Druids with their belief in reincarnation (and Christians with their teaching of The Resurrection) regarded it as an emblem of everlasting life. The Irish regarded it as one of the most ancient beings on earth. Yew is the last on a list of oldest things in a passage from the 14th century Book of Lismore: "*3 lifetimes of The Yew for the world from its beginning to its end.*"

In the Brehon Laws, it is named as one of the Seven Chieftain Trees, with heavy penalties for felling one. Staves of Yew were kept in Pagan graveyards in Ireland where they were used for measuring corpses & graves. In the Bardic schools, poets used staves to help them memorize incantations. They were also used for carving Ogham letters.

In Christian times churches built their edifices on Pagan burial grounds in Yew groves They also planted one beside the path leading from the funeral gateway of the churchyard to the main door, and the other beside the path leading to the lesser doorway.

Priests would gather under The Yew to await corpse-bearers. The remains of Anglo-Saxon churches suggest that the early English planted Yews in a circle around the church, which were usually built upon a central mound. There is also a tradition that the Christian Cross was a Yew.

The Isle of Iona, the "sacred island" of St. Columba off Scotland is said to get its name from the Gaelic word for 'Yew-tree', Ioho or Ioha. The island was once a powerful Druid centre, planted with sacred groves of Yew.

The famous Yews of Nevern in Dyfed, Wales are said to bleed a red substance every year in sympathy with the Christ. Branches of Yew were used in Palm Sunday processions instead of palm and the altars of many churches were decked with branches of Yew on Easter Day. The Yew is also associated with New Year's Day; villagers would gather beneath the churchyard Yew to celebrate.

The Yew's toxicity has limited its practical uses, though a homeopathic tincture is made of young shoots & berry to treat cystitis, headache and neuralgia. Shakespeare's Macbeth Witches bore "slips of Yew slivered in the moon's eclipse."

Shields and weaponry made from The Yew were highly admired by the Celts; the longevity was transferred to the warrior. It was used for spears, spikes, staves, small hunting bows & longbows. The arrows were tipped with poison made from The Yew. The wood is hard & bright orange – once treated, it is almost impossible to damage.

There are about 10 different species of Yew in the northern temperate zones of Asia, Asia Minor, India, Europe, North Africa & North America. They are all thought to have descended from PALEOTAXUS REDIVIVA, which was found imprinted on Triassic era fossils. Recently, more fossils of Yew have been found from the Jurassic era.

According to pollen counts, Yew trees grew in great abundance at the time of the Ice Age. As the glaciers receded northwards, the great forests of Europe contained up to 80% of Yew trees.

The Yew is considered to be the most powerful tree for protection against evil. It was thought The Otherworld would whisper through Yew staves during rituals and initiations. It is linked to Samhain, when entry to the Otherworld is mythologically easiest – when dreams & ancestors rise.

The Yew also connects through Samhain and the water element to Scorpio, ruled by Pluto. The Yew is linked to the runes YR and EOLH, both ruled by Jupiter. The Yew is also considered feminine, its element is water and planet Saturn.

A strange belief in the north of Scotland concerning The Yew was that a person, when grasping a branch of Yew in the left hand, may speak to anyone he pleases without that person being able to hear, even though everyone else present can.

Yew has also long been part of funerary customs – carrying sprigs of Yew which are either thrown in the grave, under the body or on the coffin.

Yew groves planted by The Druids were common by ancient ways, on sacred sites, hilltops, ridge ways and burial grounds. Tribal leaders were buried beneath Yew trees, in the sure belief that their knowledge and wisdom would be joined with the Dryad of The Yew and therefore still be accessible to the tribe for generations to come...

I didn't understand this was my finale with Dark Paganism and that greater options were soon forthcoming. In my research I realized The Tree Of Life & The Tarot were intertwined, and I finally cracked the story of the Magician (and Magickian).

I was transforming alongside the spiritual & psychological Alchemy research. Luminous visions overtook me; I saw the glory of The Great Work on my own terms...

I was playing in 2 bands – one was another guy's ship where I was vocalist. Weekly practices yet no shows – decent people & music, but unsure of direction. My self-controlled band? Me and a drummer, and I'd just cut off the tip of my finger at work and had to have it sewn back on. It made the tip numb from nerve damage and I had to wait months to heal.

The gay scene was a joke. I tried repeatedly for years but I was alone. It should be mentioned that the threat of contracting HIV really impacted my life. When fear & paranoia lurks upon you endlessly, it really takes the wind out of your sails. Any hook up with someone you are playing roulette with a potential gruesome death.

It wore down on all of our minds and traumatized us all. I lived an insanely guarded, unsatisfactory life because of this. Many times I met someone and things started going somewhere and then they were like "*oh, by the way...*" Ruined many potential joyous periods. AIDS was a terrifying specter.

When Truvada (Prep) became available & cheap – a drug that prevents HIV transmission at a 99% rate – everything in the gay scene changed. But not a single person told me. They just thought I knew what was up. I was oblivious to the fact that my public healthcare was just doling it out for free to anyone who asked.

I remained in the miserable funk of fearing HIV transmission that I needlessly continued wandering in, while the entire community around me got that monkey off their backs. It would be quite some time before I got on it myself – *nearly 2 years after it had become commonplace!* I'm still so angry not a person bothered to even explain it to me.

In this funk this one dude snuck up on me – a male I was actually marginally attracted to. I had forgot that this as even a possibility! As with everyone, he was a batshit crazy psycho-stalker chameleon dressing the way he was in order to lure me into his lunatic trap. He presented himself under completely false pretenses to get near me.

Eventually he stayed the night and immediately turned around and told everyone who would listen every last detail. Everything this guy lured me in with was about being low key & private. And when alone at my house he stole a page of my Yew research!

He did that thing that all these Normy's do – they see something Magickal and then something overtakes them, they see power, they see gold. And they steal it and run with it – power they don't understand and can never use or even figure out how it even works. They never even think: "*I could just Google this stuff.*" No – it has to be this instant serpentine streak of greed that overtakes them. They have to Steal the fire of Olympus, they don't know how to just go find it on their own. It's like watching SMÉAGOL warping from The One Ring.

I quickly got the stolen research back and abruptly ended anything with this loser. In response he went full-on psycho-stalker, lurking on me at my work, in public. Then started threatening to call the FBI on my house because we were throwing Punk Rock shows in the basement. This enemy of Punk Rock continued stalking me by telling people I was in an ongoing relationship with him, and we were participating in gay orgies all over the city.

My work 86'd him, he went off in his batshit direction and inevitably started stalking some other guy. For the next year I'd be walking downtown and he'd pop out acting friendly. Always trying to get back in. He was totally insane.

And then one day, standing outside a gay club downtown, someone walked up off the street and shot him twice in the head and three times in the heart. I absolutely did not care. I mean, I'm sorry the guy is dead and all, but just because someone died in a tragic way doesn't change the fact that they lived their entire life as a total prick. He was a piece of trash when he was alive and he's a piece of trash as a corpse too.

I attracted all manner of losers and psycho-stalkers, all who demanded things from me and when they did not get what they wanted they turned into hecklers, haters, saboteurs. Everything that wasn't typing about The Yew was making me miserable.

The larger problem with the band & my reputation in the scene – basically I just wandered into a bad situation they got me locally canceled in the Punk scene. I never even did anything f***ed up to anyone, I just stood there in the wrong place at the wrong time.

Some of the guys in the band I was jamming with had a side band, an anarchist Grindcore band. They had picked up this new guitarist, a nice young kid. His father wanted to see his son play live, so we gave him a ride to the show. We roll up to this anarchist house venue as a bunch of anarchists ready to have a good ol' anarchist jamboree playing Grindcore music for crusty Punk Rock Antifa kids.

What we don't know is that the father we just gave a ride to was in prison in Texas and joined a Nazi gang and had a racist tattoo on his arm. Guy walks up to the house, abruptly walks out and then scuttles down the street not saying where he was headed. These SHARP skinhead early 20's kids emerge from the house – they challenge us to a fight! They claim we are secret Nazis with a Nazi band invading their venue.

It all just happened so fast. We're in the street – one kid grabs me from behind and holds onto me, like he's bear-hugging me to keep me still. He's loosely hugging me though, he has no strength. It's just some kid. If anything happens here, I'm the one who's going to end up in prison.

No one standing there has ever been backed into a corner by people claiming they are Nazis who are also ready to physically attack them. It was shockingly stupid and there was no time to think. Never did any of us ever think we would be put in this position, and it was so absurd that as it happened we were all dazed by how impossible it seemed. None of us were even certain what to do. But it was clear that if any of us threw a first punch then everything was going to hell in a handbasket.

The other kid starts going after my buddy. Starts telling him he's a secret Nazi. My friend does everything possible to try and talk this guy out of his aggression, that this is a f***ed up mistake. We don't even know this guy, he just got a ride. He's this kid's dad.

Skinhead kid doesn't care and swings a punch on my friend. My buddy dodges it and continues trying to talk him down. Skinhead kid doesn't care – lands a punch.

My friend snaps: *"I'll show you what I think of Nazis!!"* Grabs the kid's head and throws him to the ground – starts bashing his skull into the concrete: *"This is what I think of Nazis!! This is what I think of Nazis!!!"* The kid bear-hugging me releases and staggers back in shock.

My friend though, he bashes this kids head into the concrete six times and leaves him bloody on the ground. The kid gets up dazed and both take off. We go in and play the show anyway. Nothing happens. Except off screen they've called up every single Antifa 19 year old in the city. And we have an entire army that wants to beat the living shit out of us. And all I did was stand there.

Now all the Antifa kids hate us and think we are clandestine Nazi sympathizers. Our house venue is being looked at like some secret racist band haven. However, anyone involved in the music scene who ever dealt with us knows this is absolutely not true. All I did was get a ride to a show and my reputation was destroyed. I never hurt a hair on anyone's head.

Now I have to worry about getting jumped by Antifa kids when I was Antifa back when they were in their diapers! *Before they were even conceived!* I was Old School, they just didn't know me because I was living a low profile on purpose.

Talk about being framed as the opposite of everything you are! Why? Because as a leftist anarchist radical crusty Grindcore musician from a Queer Power house venue I went to an anarchist house venue with queer anarchists to see them play? That's what cancels my career & social life? Gets me gang stalked & potentially jumped by Scene Police? It was the craziest thing that ever happened, and of course it happened to me.

With social media everyone can interject. Now I had a legion of deeply misinformed trolls framing me as a Nazi when I'm the type of person the Nazis want to kill! I was Antifa since I learned what a Nazi was! *I was the old school veteran who gave my life to the cause!*

In the blink of an eye, everything ended. I was turned into their Supervillain. An entire lifetime of activity tarnished! I was a lifer in the Punk scene and they took it away at the drop of a hat, just like all the other liars who framed me as other bad things because I refused to stick my dick inside them or wouldn't play weird games.

Nothing was more toxic an environment then so called leftist liberal Portland. They were the worst group of kids I ever encountered, in any scene, in any city, and a good thousand of them acted like a clique reigning supreme.

No one who ever knew me personally or read a book I ever penned or listened to the lyrics of any band I ever played in – they knew damn well I was certainly no Nazi. Still, Portland was ruined. They assassinated me for no reason. Well, the Witchcraft attack was coming. The gloves were off. I was again the Goblin in the 18th century woodcut...

Around this time, the Black & Jewish girl returned. I apparently really upset her. We hung out and she lunged right at me. Afterwards she told me that when I just stopped talking her she began contemplating suicide. And then I pulled out the Voodoo Zombie Slave Love Potion I got from Pagan Pride and we drank it together – we turned each other into our mutual zombies & went on a dirty marathon...

She had a rather brilliant idea which she envisioned as a way to have a decent relationship. In Portland there is a local DIY film festival where everyone shoots their own porno and then they play them at an event called HUMP. Her Grand Vision was to make a porn called "*The Dicker Man*" – it would be a Pagan Porn that would climax with a gigantic orgy inside a Wicker Man shaped like a huge erect cock. And everyone would f**k their brains out before everything (mockingly) went up in flames.

In between it would be about Witches & Druids seducing Christians and whoever else into this wild orgy, just Witches f**king all over town in a gigantic Pagan freakout. He found it hilarious but didn't quite take it serious. I mean, he could have. Anyone else would have. But guess what? It was in the way of The Tree.

This woman was pretty cool actually, but she had no grip on any of this Magick stuff. She just looked at me like I was some kooky dude. But she apparently thought I was hot shit, and why deny her? Maybe I'd open up to her eventually.

She took me to her new place and soon pulled out her S&M torture kit with all kinds of monstrous contraptions. She just laid down in front of me – like do whatever you please. I did not want to be doing this. I went softcore to make her happy, hating it the entire time.

I continued seeing this girl for the next few months. She never again brought up her trinkets or wanting to go to violent places. I wasn't pushing it, certainly. I think she wanted a real relationship with me, although I did not understand why. I kept going with it.

By early October it was time to do a European tour, but the whole thing plus my book memoir coming out that Halloween – it was all just in the way of The Tree.

We had a 5 day tour in Belgium and Germany. We bought airline tickets together, but they failed to tell me that I had to also sign up for some coupon to get the cheap deal. The band leader informed us in a group email I did not see – and he sat there with me as I booked the ticket, clearly watching me not do this and said nothing.

I get a week and half off from work. At the airport my ticket didn't work – in slow motion I ran around the hallways trying to find an ATM to withdraw all my money at the last second and buy a new one. It all fell apart, right on the spot. The second I was going to do my first European tour with a band The Big Dream collapses.

They just left me there, 3 hours from home in Seattle at the airport. I took a bus to my old stomping grounds – fare $3. I remembered my ex girlfriend Miss 3 cursing me from when we lived in Seattle. It was $3 to take bus from airport. 3 ravens outside the burger joint. The bus home was $33. I was done with them.

I just remember the whirl of trees outside the Greyhound window. I felt hardcore Witchy and all I wanted was to get back to my Yew Info Comp so I could unleash this new Pagan idol of worship upon the Magick underground. I had fully returned to the woods. Wanted to climb into a house of wattles and clay.

I thought of my current girlfriend. Before I left on tour she said, *"Once you get back, Mister, we're going to a motel and I want you to BLEEEEEEEP."* Anyone else would have ran to her. But she was in the way of The Tree.

I thought of all the women in Europe I had once fallen for, and the one above all others that I lost. I still saw her out the corner of my eye so often. I had hoped she would appear somehow at one of our gigs, though I knew it was a fantasy. I lost the one I loved above all, and it was a story only for me, because not a person connected to my life ever knew her. But would she understand The Tree?

I thought about how I should have just ditched the USA and stayed homeless in Europe for years. Had I made the wrong decision? It seems the only right decision was to resurrect The Witches Tree. Yggdrasil was returning to The Earth.

I plowed into a week straight of typing. By the time the band was back the book was done – 666 pages with aggressive launching. Every single Facebook group, forum, website I could find. Every Twitter, every media account, all my PR contacts – just this monster blitzkrieg. I felt like Conal Cochran from *Halloween 3*. Can't make heads melt with snakes & cockroaches but I can resurrect The Tree of Death.

No one seemed to know what to think unless they were deep into Magick. I can't even imagine what my Antifa stalkers must have thought. More then anything people were alienated because people are only your friends as long as they see themselves in you. No one was remotely expecting me to be so fanatic about Paganism, Witchcraft and psychic hallucinogenic trees.

This is when Holly was found dead in the river. It just kind of happened. One day she was there, the next she was gone. I remember last I seen her. Broke up with her boyfriend while in town, and she came straight over. Right then and there could have stopped. But I couldn't stop typing my Yew thing – I was 420 pages in. Told her to stay at my place while I was at work. I came home with a 24 pack of beer cans. I was going to make love to her, tell her to stay, but she was already gone.

9 months later, traveling with that same guy they found dead in river, and the security camera has them arguing at store. Cops questioned him briefly and he fled. No evidence, no witness, no charges – don't even know the guys name. Cops didn't care. Treated her like a vagrant but she was a college student with a loving family. She left her travelpack on the road and a cardboard sign to wave down drivers that read "Free Shrugs." That was it.

She had broke up with her boyfriend and was shrugging her way back to me. I know it. She had talked about coming back there after traveling it was inevitable. But whatever happened, happened. Whether she went to take a piss and fell down the hill and drowned, or whether her angry boyfriend pushed her in – no answer. No clue.

The freakiest thing is she always told me she thought she would be whacked by a serial killer while hitchhiking Oregon. That was her self prophecy. She talked about serial killers hunting those areas. I mean, is that what happened? All of this is horrible to consaider.

I don't remember crying. I still don't even really feel it. It's like a distant echo. We were on and off for 9 years. She lived in Washington and I in Portland, we would see each other maybe every year. We would always be together. We just never talked about it or confronted it. The last thing she did was talk to me on the phone. The last thing she said "*I always enjoy my [insert name here] time*" and she was gone forever.

The Pagan Freakout had started – The Yew was striking Portland as if a Daikaiju. In the hustle, this girl shows up I barely knew who had been to a few shows at our house. She was a lifelong junkie now homeless & sleeping outdoors in the snow. She was about ready to die and had nowhere to go.

When I thought of her I could only envision Natalie Portman in *The Professional,* standing outside the hitman's door begging to be let in. I said to myself, "*if you don't, this one is dead.*" So I opened the door and let her in. Little did I know she thought of me like Leon, with my little plant in my little room.

She slept on the couch for 3 days, barely awake & regenerating. Afterwards she just never left. She was one of the most agreeable people I ever met. Autistic and childlike, all she wanted to do was eat cereal and watch cartoons. I was able to give her the room downstairs.

Within 2 months we all got evicted. It was time to go mobile – just myself and the girl. First we got a condemned trailer for $200. Harassed by cops, we'd tow it block to block. This lasts maybe 3 weeks. Next we got a little red van named Clifford.

We just sailed away like pirates in our pirate ship and had our own little world. Just movies & Comic Books & cotton candy & Sweet Tarts & licorice & George Romero & Pro Wrestling & all the dankest weed we could ever smoke in the stoner capital of the Northwest. It went on & on like this for years. I was finally happy…

Pale White Horsey

By the way, here is your future – 440+ days until the vaccine goes in your arm, and 1,067 days until you get off The Street. Combined to the 824 days of homelessness you already spent between May 2017 & March 2020. Welcome to The Global Pandemic there Buddy Boy – confetti just exploding in every direction…

Years ago, the skeptical drummer of my old band had unveiled his prophecy. Our act was centered around exploring conspiracies through ripping Grindcore. He told me: *"None of these conspiracies you're screaming about are remotely legit – not HAARP, not FEMA Camps, Morgellons or Chemtrails. You want to write about something real? How about we do a concept album where something like SARS got out. Now that's some real shit right there – the world would fall apart in an instant, cause that's The Fart Plague."*

"All it would take is one guy making it to a public toilet in a major city and the world would be doomed. Every toilet would be like a deadly gas chamber – that virus lives forever on all surfaces too. It's The Fart Plague because it's mainly spread by gas and the little shit follicles when we take a dump. Every bathroom is like a snow globe of poop particles you shake up. Except you are the horsey in the middle."

"You'd never be able to shit in a public toilet ever again, or touch anything at the supermarket, eat anything, or handle money. That shit is pretty lethal – all it would have to do is make it to some place like a Gym Shower or a Gay Bathhouse and we'd be f**ked."

He proposed to do a concept album and we came up with "Fart Plague." It would literally about the world falling apart from SARS like a hellscape and the title would also describe our music. SARS was a conspiracy to be reckoned with.

This is why the very second I caught wind of COVID that my entire world changed. I just slipped into that Doomsday Prepper mindset where you have to take control of the situation and act accordingly. It's dead serious and you are surrounded by people who have no idea what was going on or how to respond or navigate with no public info campaign.

The Authorities didn't want people panicking so they would only give out information bit by bit. That way at least the smart people would figure it out, because the common person couldn't. And this is what I'm talking about – when you're one of the Smart Ones who had the foresight to see deep into the future of what this would actually look like.

Yet POW – you're surrounded by a vast mass who are absolutely clueless and could not see past the next couple days. The people that could see were those who had money, homes, good jobs – doctors & lawyers & college educated people. Then there's folks like Dr. Zeero who are just living in a van working as a dishwasher at a pizza place.

It was the day after the helicopter crash with Kobe Bryant. I was waiting to pay the bill at Denny's where I'd just devoured a strawberry banana pancake dinner. I was gazing at my phone on CNN's website, just scrolling down. I'm like *"Kobe died"* and then I scroll down more – *quarantine in China.* That meant they couldn't control it anymore and it had broken through. Chinese Lunar New Year celebrations just happened – masses of infected were flying out into the world. Then, oh, by the way it's this freakish, mysterious, unknown strain of Mega SARS – a likely bio-weapon from a lab leak.

My entire reality flipped. I was immediately living in the ultimate conspiracy of my oldschool band. I was happily just living and hanging out with the autistic Witchy girl. We'd play with Tarot cards & collect crystals & read Magick books & hang out in nature. It was just me and her and a little black cat for years. Just being left alone in our own little world waiting for the Trump years to end.

I took one look at that phone and saw the future. I explained to her it's already broken out, it's already in our city – we immediately have to start isolating & wearing masks & gloves. Secondly, we need to stock up on food because it isn't safe for farm workers or meat processing plant workers to be standing side by side. There's going to be food shortages. Furthermore, neither of us will be able to work anymore either.

Then there was all this insane stuff about how people were dropping dead in seizures on TikTok. Just BAM – you can't use a public toilet anymore. There's no vaccine and there won't be for a very long time (if ever). This virus is killing people & making them go into convulsions & making their brains swell up. We aren't being given the mortality rate by the Chinese because we can't really trust an authoritarian government to give us true data.

The Doomsday Prepper sort of dude in me, that militant guy immediately took over. I'm thinking: *"Oh this girl – smart person, she's going to take this serious."* As soon as we get on the train there's someone hacking their lungs out. He's like, *"I'm sick, I'm sick..."* She just runs right up to him, gets in his breathing space – touching him and trying to tell him how to get to the hospital. Did not compute.

It was clear that she was going to get me killed or nightmare sick. Furthermore, if we get sick we give it to other people and it's a chain of death or extreme misery. We were potential walking death to those with vulnerable health conditions.

That week I jumped up & down like a man screaming on fire trying to convince this girl all of this was really happening. Her response was thinking I was over-exaggerating and totally paranoid. She was completely annoyed by me, basically. She would not change her habits or interface with the world surrounding her.

It was life or death. We could no longer touch money, breathe air – no toilet, no handmade food, no cigarette halfies off the ground. No touching items in stores without gloves, no taking money from people – must spray purchased items with bleach water, roll a scarf over your mask like a Ninja, wear goggles inside businesses. This virus lived 4 days on wood & organic material, lives weeks on plastic. The colder it is the longer it lives...

They said you would know the virus by the metallic taste in your mouth and a severe & strange headache. Then you would feel like you were getting violently ill. At that point either it would seemingly recede, it would magnify horribly, or you'd potentially go into shock and drop dead. Or your lungs would inflame and you'd be hooked to a ventilator.

Within days this episode of illness happened to me. We were both mutually sick with headaches. She slept through most of it whereas I woke up at night feeling like I was going to die. I crept from the vehicle and into the bushes, dropping to my knees. My whole body was weak and my bones felt icy. I began vomiting.

I said to myself, *"Is this it? Am I about to drop dead?"* POOF – normal again. It just went away after a few quick pukes. Was it Covid or a simple head cold? I was in denial and unsure. But I knew I was likely a carrier, or could be, and I was pretending that I wasn't but not quite sure. This experience also probably happened to every single person in the city, all over the nation as well.

I showed up to work in denial. We would be closing up the shop fairly soon, that part was obvious. This is the frame of time before March 19th, when all the shops and businesses everywhere closed down and laid off their employees. It was maybe 3 days left.

Long story short, there was no hope she could operate as needed in the situation. I tried vigorously but I couldn't convince her. I had to break off and isolate. I knew I was probably infectious and had to be away from all people. So I went to stay at the band rehearsal space I was still renting even though my band had broken up a year ago.

I couldn't sleep there or keep food there, so I had to constantly sleep outside every night. I got lucky because there was a small patch of nature behind a lawyer's office that was only open from 10pm to 5pm. It was a spot that must have been used for junkies to shoot up for many years.

Since everything had closed down there was no other homeless around really – not a single place to hang out & charge your phone. No coffee shop, no fast food place, nowhere to return bottles, no toilet. It was a dead zone of factories near a railyard.

Plus it was far away from the epicenter of dope and meth dealers in Portland. I was basically the only homeless guy in the area, except for some folks living in their cars. The managers of the practice space were always on my ass, but I never broke the rules. Even if I was shitting in bags in my own room because I couldn't use their toilets (sorry guys).

In any instance, I had turned the hidden nature section into my latrine. I was camping down there and occasionally showering there; I had one of those plastic portable shower bags. I'd fill it with hot water from the gas station across the street and hang it off the pine tree. That place was my savior – tiny gas station with a dinky parking lot and large shady tree. I sat there day after day contemplating the future.

The first day that I retreated into my rehearsal space like a bunker was when the Governor's emergency orders were being enforced. We were in a State of Emergency with "Shelter In Place" laws enacted. Now it was legal to just set up a tent anywhere you wanted, in a state where every drug was decriminalized. Portland was fast crumbling into the world I had always wanted it to be.

I remember shutting the door behind me at that fateful moment. Just hearing sirens in the distance, all manner of commotion & dogs barking. I barricaded myself inside. I knew the world I was born into was done for. There would be only life before and after Covid. We'd probably never even find a vaccine. The world was a ticking time bomb sure to eventually rip itself apart. I laid down on the ground and began sobbing. I was alone again.

There I was, a $265 a month room as long as my savings held out. I knew I was doomed to the street, so I had to get all my affairs in order. Shut down shop on Portland completely – put out every last album & book I ever wrote. Send all my books to every Magick & Witchcraft & Occult bookstore in America – and the most important European shops as well.

I was confined to a small terrain of a handful of blocks and endless clueless Americans. Just a 7-11 & a gas station. Everything was closed and the church security threatened me with arrest for sleeping under its awning. Same as Reed College.

It was the Ninja who saved me. The second I sealed myself into the rehearsal space, the book awaiting me was *Mind Of The Ninja*. I devoured it and immediately searched out Stephen K. Hayes. I watched every Ninja related thing on YouTube I could find. I ordered every major Ninja book used off eBay. Only with their guidance could I walk through this Valley of the Shadow of Death. I learned to merge with the shadows...

During this research, Covid had killed my aunt. She was in a convalescent center because of Alzheimer's. I knew that a chunk of change would eventually come my way, but I wasn't so concerned. I was fairly fond of this relative, despite some ugly things she said in life. I felt bad for her, but she also would have wanted to be painlessly out of her misery.

Since shopping indoors breathing the same air as other people was potentially deadly – and believing the supply chains would eventually break down – I began buying hundreds of dollars of canned goods & burying vacuum sealed stashes in parks around town. Since I had to eventually move out of my practice space I also had to bury chunks of my book collection, tools, etc underground. I had caches all over the city.

The streets of Portland were full of desperate individuals. I didn't want to travel outside my safe zone; I had to avoid all people. It was clear that the only ones left now were those who really wanted to be here. When an event like Covid happens, all the transplants from elsewhere just fold and go back to their families. Portland was more pure then it ever had been in this respect.

There was a severe moment of Microcosm & Macrocosm involving a bickering couple. As I tried to sleep in my little nature cove one night, I heard a couple arguing in the nearby parking lot. They had just moved to Portland from out of state and were stuck living in their car, because the plague destroyed their plans.

He was trying to console her, but every bit of his tongue held back, "*Shut up you f**king bitch.*" I crept up to them because they were screaming at each other about being hungry and that there was no money. So I waved and set down a generic can of SPAM.

Soon as I returned to my wooden palette bed & plastic tarp blanket, I heard them fighting like raccoons over trash. They were playing tug of war with a SPAM can! He won and ran off from her, abandoning the girl and the car. She was cursing him, screaming into the night. She started sobbing and slammed the car door to huff & puff alone in the vehicle. It was representative on a small scale of what was going on out there. If that was the deal with them, then it was the same with similar situations.

Speaking of Microcosm/Macrocosm, we need to talk about FEMA. This next part people with think I'm tripping, but I watched FEMA melt away into nothingness with my own eyes. And if they disintegrated in Portland, it was everywhere else too.

This scene came around the moment that I consciously realized I hadn't seen a single cop in 2 months. They too were fearful of getting sick, and like every other house dwelling person they took the stance of "tough shit."

The cops couldn't maintain any of this anyway. The entire city & nation had fallen. The only thing holding it together was the power of denial, the potentially false hope of a vaccine, and that people have been psychologically conditioned to just keep showing up to work and paying bills, no matter the situation.

The Government had no way to control the situation but were obliged to pretend. The National Emergency had been declared. However, the stockade of medical equipment that Obama had sequestered to deal with a medical emergency at a national level like this – they only had enough to where they could take care of one state. In an apocalyptic scenario, they could handle something the size of New York. They were caught unprepared with no idea what to do.

Now this part – I don't know if this was FEMA or another federal agency, but this was certainly a Trump directive. They declared "we're going to help the homeless people" so they made rescue stations for the homeless – sports auditoriums & convention centers as sanctuaries. At our Convention Center they had made large Tic-Tac-Toe rectangles on the floor with masking tape – like little boxes all scrunched next to each other. Those were all for the homeless people to sleep on mats.

While they didn't "round up the homeless" to try and blatantly kill them – they certainly set the death trap and then aggressively informed the homeless to come for shelter. So in the middle of this deadly pandemic, they force a bunch of people to all crowd next to each other in scrunched up little boxes, all breathing the same air? Why else would you do such a thing unless you were trying to spread plague on purpose? What else would be the point except exterminating whoever you could? What's the difference between this action and a toxic gas chamber?

It was coordinated nationwide – President Chump tried to murder as many homeless as he could. Bullshit he was ignorant of this plan. Nobody's talking about it but it absolutely happened. I know it did, because I was one of the targets they tried to fool into killing myself with their little plague chamber. Scum.

Anyhow, FEMA had areas selected where in case of an emergency they could set up shop at a predetermined location. I swear up & down that the little Warehouse section I was living in – all those empty warehouses never used for anything – all of a sudden the entire area was packed with white unmarked cars. The apartment that was always vacant – all of a sudden dozens of identical model white cars.

Standing on the corner I see 3 cops on motorcycles that are a motorcade leading a semi truck with a flat attached to it that is hauling a small command post on wheels, like a trailer from a trailer park. The nervous driver looked me in the eyes and he knew that I knew what was going on. The cops escorted it down the street and must have just opened one of the unoccupied warehouse garages that had previously sat there like empty, dead buildings.

They just wheeled it inside – all of a sudden it's like BOOM this whole area comes alive from April to July. Then on July 1st – POOF – all the places were shut down & vacant. All the white cars were gone. Everything got fenced up. Ghost Town. I knew we were in a hopeless situation. FEMA buckled under and left us to our own devices.

When I looked online there were videographers all over the USA who had filmed exactly what I saw, with authorities ushering white trailer command posts on the back of semi truck rigs. About how FEMA was setting up in their area. I know what I saw...

Things were like walking a tightrope financially, because there simply was no working a job nor would there be for some time. I had what I had and that was that. When it ran out I would be picking cans with thousands of desperate street people as competition.

Furthermore, the large amount of homeless people & street junkies made all the stores change their return policies. You could only get $2.40 worth of bottle returns per day at most major supermarkets. And all the 7-11 type places – $5 a day, that's it.

Only a few years ago, all these had a limit of $30+ a day. All the shysters had abused the system by manipulating the bottle return slips the workers would write up, forging different cash amounts & printing fake return tickets & selling them to other junkies lingering outside supermarkets. Greedy f**kers ruined it for everyone.

My final paycheck plus what I had saved up left me with around 2 grand. I got extremely lucky with my tax returns and got $1,200 back – plus both of the Trump stimulus checks. Living off canned food and smoking the cheapest cigars on the market, I knew I could drag it out until deep winter, maybe even spring.

Global Civilization had drifted into a slow burn *Mad Max*. The one joy I'd discovered was training with throwing knives. I dragged a wooden palette indoors and used it for constant target practice. I became lethal in my precision.

The one thing that kind of surprised me (but not really) – when you take away sporting events, concerts, jobs, TV shows, ability to go to movies, ability to make money... protesting becomes the new sport & hobby of the population. This is what made the George Floyd protests hit critical mass.

The city exploded into massive protests that no one could hold back. All of downtown – windows boarded, spray paint everywhere. Fences protecting business. Barricades around the court house, police station, City Hall – and all those building spray painted with "f**k pigs" sloganeering.

There were tens of thousands who had poured onto the streets. Helicopters flooded the sky, cops in riot gear driving tank-like vehicles through the city. To the point where Homeland Security arrived like a military force – and ended up tear gassing our own mayor! All who were eventually chased off by a naked dancing woman in the street.

While our city exploded in a tangled mess, I hid from it all. I remember being in my nature cover, hearing sirens wail in the distance. Knowing Homeland Security had come to round up and arrest suspected "Antifa" or specific protesters.

I felt like a chump for hiding, but Covid had just killed my aunt and I had the same genetics. I could not risk it, no matter how amazing the spectacle. You cannot understand how much self control it took to just stay seated in my little Spider Hole. It's what I always wanted to see – the epic crescendo was here. Yet here I was hiding like a rat because it wasn't safe to go near people.

I didn't care if people thought I was a coward. I'd proven my bravery many times in demonstrations. This was the one occasion everyone had to stand up for the vulnerable who could not participate. Folks with Vitamin D deficiency were getting destroyed by Covid. I felt like Travolta in *Boy In The Plastic Bubble*.

After the bustle of the biggest mass protests the city had ever seen, Downtown was Post Apocalyptic. Tents were everywhere – you could just pop one anywhere you wanted. The cops were totally invisible. No sanctuary at churches; they were all closed too. People living in cars everywhere.

I realized at this point just how nonsensical people were about the potential of a vaccine. Nothing had even been announced and people were rejecting it outright, as if a conspiracy. I mean, if you tell someone that they will get a virus that makes their dick rot off, they would run to the vaccine immediately. If you say it kills them? They just Shrug. This is how I learned that most Americans do not understand what death is. They don't understand that not only does your cock rot off, your entire body rots off. You rot off!

By November I was running out of money; Thanksgiving 2020 I went homeless and reunited with the girl. She was parked down in the railyard. I set up a tent next to her and things were dandy. Unlike other homeless we had a gas generator saving our asses + dozens of portable chargers fired up to the max. Our phones were always tip-top charged.

I still had the massive collection of unread Magick & Occult & Witchcraft books I had been stockading before this mess began. I could finally just dig into my research. Luckily I had an ex girlfriend letting me keep my books in her shed.

Soon a good dozen tweekers found our spot and invaded, parking all around us & setting up tents. They were all junkies & thieves too. Couldn't trust any of them or leave possessions unguarded. One of them had broke into my friends vehicle and lifted $200. My best portable charger also randomly disappeared.

Well, there I was, stinky homeless guy underneath several sweaters, hoodies, coats growing a gigantic scraggly red beard because I had no access to a shower or anywhere to shave. And there were giant rats everywhere. All night they'd swirl around my tent like a tornado. If I opened my tent zipper, they would just lunge in and I'd have to chase them out. One night, when it was 20 degrees, I was so god damn tired I just fell asleep again with this rat in my tent. I woke up after 15 minutes, realized what I was doing & got him out of there.

Towards the end of winter I was very bored & distant. I kept soldiering forth, but when you walk the same ground day after day in purgatory things gets old. You just want to scream. I mean, I had family from my home state offering to come back there and stay with them. But it was dangerous – none of those people could operate as needed in the face of Covid. They would get me sick and kill me.

There was this huge empty mall nearby that used to be a beacon of light for the homeless. You could once park there all day, charge your phone from electrical sockets + they had multiple toilets. But now all the outlets were plugged up, security would chase you out if you dozed off in one of the leather cushioned chairs in the hallways.

All the toilets were closed except one, and it stunk like the elephant exhibit at the zoo. That was the only public toilet for all of North Portland. The only other public toilets? Downtown, a little metal enclosure. Both at the junkie parks. Good luck ever getting in there to piss or shit. It's just a line of intravenous drug users waiting to shoot up or smoke fentanyl or meth and there is never any toilet paper anyway.

The thing that separated the men from the boys is being able to just shit in plastic bags and throw them in whatever dumpster or public trash can you could find. Covid spread by shit, remember. I got so used to shitting in bags and in holes in the ground that it was second nature to me.

Anyway, I used to wander this empty dead mall all day, just laps around it trying to stay warm. The mall was one of the earliest indoor shopping centers in the USA. It had an ice rink and everything. It was very similar to the Monroeville Mall of *Dawn of the Dead* fame. I'd listen to the *Dawn* soundtrack repeatedly on my headphones, just "The Gonk" on repeat.

The vaccine was eventually declared open to the public. In May 2021 – after 14 months of hopelessness & homelessness – it finally went into my arm. I said, *"All right, I made it out of the nightmare – it's not like 'Escape From New York' anymore. I don't have to keep being Snake Plissken."* Well Snake, you know – he's just dumped into New York and has to make it through 24 hours. Try thousands.

Soon the cops busted up our Tweeker Town in the railyard and chased everyone out. We drove 2 blocks away to a small parking lot. As we approached an Old Man was standing in the lot – he owned it. My friend said, *"If you let me park here, I will work free as a security guard for you and chase out anyone who tries to camp."* She was tiny & harmless looking, so he said *"yes"* in a heartbeat.

He took off, I walked up, and just like that we had been granted out own chunk of land where no one else would bother us and it had all the nature necessary to build a latrine. A short walk down the street was the Max Train – a short walk up the street the only coffee shop / bakery left where you could just plug your phone in all day long, from 8am until 6pm. Both spots became my new home.

Had my aunt not died from Covid, I wouldn't have a dime. When I was approaching what must have been my last $100 I got an inheritance kickback. It wasn't a staggering amount mind you – a few thousand dollars. But considering I was living on $5 a day or less, I was one lucky man. I was Street Rich and this was going to last a very, very long time.

I said, *"F**k it – the vax is in my arm, we have our campground, and I'm on vacation until the world comes back. Y'all can go f**k yourselves."* Soon after, it was admitted that the vax was a buffer only partially stopping the virus – we had all been turned into a carrier population, due to the sheer infectiousness of it. We would need permanent upgrade shots every year, just like seasonal flu.

There were those who Covid did nothing to and were lucky in the game of genetic roulette – and there were those whom the plague would kill or otherwise destroy. An entire segment of the world population could not really live in this new world. They would be trampled under and it was abundantly clear. Victims of change.

Even though I was on Truvada & had the vax, there was no going back to hook ups on Grindr or attending gay bathhouses. When I looked at people, all I now saw were germs. All bodily fluids were poison. When I saw a mouth it was just a wet cave of Covid. The virus had turned me asexual and rendered all physical touch cringe. I stopped caring about intimacy – the last of it was beaten out of me. Who would ever want to make out with some dirty homeless guy anyway, with his red wily beard?

Time passed majestically. Got along with the girl fantastically – again we had our own private world. She lived in her bus and I lived in my tent. Back to Pro Wrestling, Tarot Cards, collecting crystals & simple Witchy pleasures. At the bakery I kept watching Magick channels on YouTube and especially the Infomercial Satan Guy. I was determined not to do a Magick book but launch my own YouTube show instead.

I began painting landscapes at the park following Bob Ross on his old shows. I would mimic the dude with the perm & soft voice; I was getting good at it. But then one day I started painting a landscape and dark images from my past seeped out. It killed my inertia.

I was tired of not participating in Witchcraft ritual. All the content creators were constantly having rituals to Deities, so why not? I had made a shrine to the mysterious God of the Ninja Fudo Myoo. I had this cauldron filled with burning incense & herb bundles. I had painted Fudo Myoo as well just to hone my focus.

Before me, in a half vision, I saw Fudo like a giant with blue skin. I asked to be shown what it had to show me. Maybe this is the moment that I truly started going off the rails. Because all I wished for started to come to me in visions...

It must have been early October when it started. Now, this part of the tale will be uncomfortable for some people, but it's what happened. I began hallucinating someone.

See, this Fudo Myoo experiment had loosed me up to this whole thing of Ritual Magick – invoking, evoking. I was getting more manic, like a rocket ship taking off. All this Magick stuff was enthusiasm & extreme faith & wonder – I could really feel it and was alight. All the other YouTube people, they were like distant friends on the same path. I had to start a channel. But how could I best the Infomercial Satan King?

I was watching clips from *The Dark Knight*. Movie of our generation – biggest comic movie of all time, seen it 100 times. Well, I was extremely spacey & exhausted. I left the bakery and stopped at the park. Exceptionally hazy, kind of foggy gray overcast...

Start thinking about Heath Ledger. I had visions of him dead in his hotel room from the overdose. I thought, *"What if I went in person to try to exorcise his ghost? What if his remnants are still trapped there?"*

I began watching news clips from when he perished. *Only 28!* Such a tragedy. We had the same birthday and when I watch his mannerisms just as a normal guy – if I had an older brother it would probably look something like him. And with *Brokeback Mountain* his portrayal of a conflicted gay man is the only one I've ever seen filmed that I could remotely recognize myself in.

And when he played Joker, he wasn't even the classic Joker from the comics but a new monster entirely – basically just projecting whatever I become deep in LSD or mushroom land. This is why I understood this Joker character intensely. It was just like a deranged, violent version of me in the depths of a monster trip.

I had heard there was a backstory for the character that Christopher Nolan & Heath Ledger came up with that they never filmed. When Ledger died Nolan just left it alone.

Anyway, I am sorry to the family of Heath Ledger if anyone connected to him actually reads this book, but this is the truth of how my mental illness went off. The next day I was at the bakery coffee shop looking at my phone, doing YouTube video watching, and I just kind of looked up and... there he was, seated before me. Half there, half invisible – I was hallucinating the ghost of Heath Ledger.

He was disheveled in his Joker outfit like it was buried with him in the grave, his face paint almost all but removed & flaking off except for slight traces. And his ghost was before me as if I was the only one who could figure out this riddle and the truth of the movie because he couldn't tell The Joke because if he did The Joke wasn't funny. So I had to decipher it. And he just stared back at me silently. And then he was gone.

I began having deep analyzing thoughts trying to pick apart the essence of the Joker character. In his essence were the keys. So I began watching the movie for clues, and it all came to me...

I think it was that night when I woke up and Heath was outside my tent, like the Jackal on The Moon Trump of Tarot. Guarding my camp, looking at the moon silently. Waiting for me to figure out the character & true movie so his soul could finally rest. Then POOF – he was gone, like rustling leaves in a quiet gust of wind.

Deeper into the movie, this whole wild back story was unveiled to me, as if living partial visions & reality at once. Joker's father slashed his face on one side (as he explained in the movie) – which means that Joker was really the first Two-Face, because he didn't complete the scarred smile until the mob carved up his wife.

Therefore, in the mental institutions he grows up in they call him "Two Face." Eventually he gets out and obviously he loves the Tarot Cards. But so does the girl he meets – what becomes his wife. It's how they connected. She looks beyond his scarred face. He also loves the Amusement Park – it becomes their special place. The relationship is based around the Carousel, and on the Carousel he always hears "London Bridge Is Falling Down."

She gets in deep with gambling, he gets dogs to protect her but the mob abducts her anyway. I have a vision of this man with his half sliced face, with his dogs chasing the mob car zooming off that nabbed his wife. He was just a dog chasing cars.

The mob slices her face just like him, but just one side of her face. That way, when they stand together it makes one long scarred smile. It ruins the Lovers Trump for him and the entire Tarot deck by default – all he can see is both of their fates in the card. A nude couple standing side by side, with one gruesome shared smile.

So he goes the next step – puts a razor in his mouth and completes the smile. But she can't stand the sight of him & leaves him. In response, he goes after the mob for revenge. As is his whole motivation in the movie. It's never about Batman – he's just fronting to fool the Mob so he can get close enough to bump them off one by one. *He's helping Batman!* Because he was inspired to act, same as those fake Batmen from the start of the film wearing hockey pads.

It was like watching a man be martyred and I began crying in the bakery. Heath dissipated again. All the Tarot connections – just started seeing it. Now if you watch the movie looking for Tarot references they just ooze off the screen. There are dozens of potential mentions. Also, all 4 suits of Tarot correspond to the 4 main factions in the film – the Maroni faction are the Coins, the Gamble faction Wands, Cups for Bruce Wayne & High Society + Swords for the Police.

All the court cards aligned with these factions, and there was a character perfect for each slot. Yet Batman himself is not part of the design – it screws up the whole thing. It only makes sense if Harvey is Batman, which Joker thought anyway, because he would be the White Knight of Swords.

I started realizing Joker was speaking Triple speak. For instance, he would be directly answering something going on, the second layer would be the bad joke he was making, then the third meaning on top of it all was a Tarot reference. The whole script became illuminated to me in this Triple Tarot Speak.

Next day I have visions of Tarot Joker as The Hanged Man – this is why only lint was in his pockets. The silver of Judas Iscariot fell out when hung upside down. It all made sense – the Tarot Joker was the fanatic of the upside down Tarot deck, and he was forcing everyone into The Game. Just pushing them into reverse Tarot land.

The Joker wasn't The Fool, he was The Magician. I didn't realize it then... but I was turning into what he was showing me. I was slowly becoming this Tarot Joker and I didn't understand. But then Heath Ledger just went away. I figured out his secret message, and he vanished. I set his soul free, privately. It was very real to me, but I wasn't telling anybody...

It was November 2021. I had been listening to the Infomercial Satan Guy a great deal. My morning routine was ASMR spine cracking videos, pimple popping videos, Bob Ross, Pro Wrestling & people ranting about Satan.

There was Satan Dude, the big dumdum. Now he was insisting that the 9 Demonic Gatekeepers lived inside him and as if the Anti-Pope you could pay him thousands of dollars and he would bless you with these demons. Then they would be transferred to you and live inside you, but through him. You'd rub his belly like the Buddha Man-Lilith and out would pop a demon. He had made amulets to send to anyone who joined his program, so they could be connected with his demonic army.

So he posts this video – a message to all of his 90,000 subscribers – that the years-long 9 Demonic Gatekeepers Ritual is complete. He had built this electronic contraption called an "Alchemite Machine" that was hooked to all kinds of radionics boxes & snow channels on old rabbit eared TVs. This pyramid of Organite, salt, sulphur, mercury + his own blood. He claimed that flipping the switch would empower all the amulets to work. And like a madman he flipped the switch and began cackling like Emperor Plapatine while wearing a Sith Lord-like black wizard hooded robe.

But then the feed cut and it went black. His channel was erased by the YouTube censors and taken offline. Why? I wasn't sure. But I was there the very moment they pulled the plug, and I was laughing like Emperor Palpatine right with him on the corner, because it was like his Conal Cochran flavored *Halloween 3* attack upon the world.

I mentioned this already, but dimwit wrote a book where it instructs you how to sacrifice someone in the name of the demon Lucifuge Rofocale to gain it's supposed favor. And a crazy person got the book and murdered 2 women. I was totally oblivious to this. His show was a ticking clock until cancellation.

The BBC had attacked him, news media all over the world. He had made us all look bad and potentially started a new Satanic Panic like in the 80's. He made my life harder and everyone's lives harder by default.

So I sat down outside an empty business at night, hit record, and ranted to YouTube. It was the start of my show – walking up to the Black Magick Mafia like Joker does the mob when he does the pencil trick. I just hit their hornets nest with a baseball bat, ranting like Ash from *Evil Dead* out to manipulate their uneasiness. I got a great deal of attention and views, but most importantly, Dr. Zeero was born. I had found my voice.

About 20 shows into the Dr. Zeero Xiron Free Magick Secrets Show it was January 2022. I was still homeless in a tent in the parking lot. Same thing every day – bakery, social media, back to camp to watch corny old movies & play with a feisty cat.

This particular night the hidden "other movie" of *The Dark Knight* unfurled to me. Lilith & Poison Ivy had united into one gnosis being. Two-Face was the husband and Poison Ivy was giving birth to demons, the first of which was Clayface. Clayface had his face carved into a smile from Two-Face in a bizarre nightmare show of parental abuse.

Clayface was turned into a martyr figure and it was revealed that all the characters in the movie – half the time it was really Clayface posing as them. When Harvey fell off the building and died at the end, it was really Clayface covering for him.

Harvey was really at Arkham driving patients insane with Scarecrow until the souls were broken and could be replaced by demonic possession. This is where all the crazy guys in black that Joker uses as his own strike force are coming from. Two-Face was straight up Satanic – and Clayface was really a Jewish Golem animated by the word EMETH.

I woke up next morning with visions of the opening bank robbery scene. The Nolan brothers had sold their souls to The Devil to make this movie happen. In return they were sold out, the production hijacked. Literally – Lucifer was Joker and letting his presence be known to all of Hollywood. Everyone in Los Angeles knew the Nolan Bros were dead but had to maintain silence. Supernatural characters had stepped in and filmed the rest of the movie! *Satan was now the star of the motion picture!*

I went to the bakery again and watched tons of scenes – all the Qabbalistic and Tarot references were illuminated and unveiling themselves rapid fire. Batman was The Hand of God and Joker wanted God to punish him. That's why he kept shouting, "*Hit me! Hit me!*" as Batman rode towards him on a motorcycle.

I found the website of the screenplay writer David S. Goyer. I sent an email full of all the coded references I could find and applauded him for his Qabbalistic screenplay. I knew this was true because I asked for a sign. Since he was from Michigan and was a writer I asked the Tarot to prove what I was thinking. Out flew the Ace of Wands as I shuffled – a giant hand that was like the mit of Michigan and a wand that was like a pencil because he was a writer. It was all the proof I needed.

I went back to camp with the girl, and we had to go to the department store / supermarket. On the drive she mentioned someone had been found dead on the side of the road years ago. It was totally unconnected to anything involving us, but I thought she was warning me about the aliens we were going to encounter at Fred Meyers. She was trying to tell me she was really an alien through coded messages before we got there.

At the store she slipped off into the back area to enter an intergalactic portal where she would be recalled to her planet and replaced with a clone. I was losing her for this clone I now would have to watch, because it was an alien invading our world.

The lights were daunting inside, so I went out into the parking lot. I was now Commissioner Gordon on the curb. I had to somehow convince the entire police department there was an alien invasion. Someone pulled up and tried to give me a $20 bill, but I was sure there was a virus on it that would scramble my DNA. I refused to take it.

Back at camp she showed me the Netflix cartoon *Arcane*. The cast of *Arcane* was really my family and shes really a space queen trying to jog my memory of what my life really is. She was involved during Occupy disappearing people I knew. She had been part of an alien plot to attempt to kill many of my friends.

I wake up the next day and go to the get coffee from the corner store – the streets were empty. I was convinced it was 10,000 years in the future now, and that all the people were robots or aliens posing as people. Back at camp I was convinced she was using hypodermic needles to withdraw purple liquid from her neck and distributing these vials to other aliens in the city, because they need it like sustenance to continue living. They needed it same as we need air.

I went to the bakery and back to camp. I was being filmed like *Truman Show* and broadcast to multiple alien worlds. I had to fake out the camera and did a strange dance throwing my Rider Waite cards into the air all over the parking lot. After all, they were planning to send every machine on earth to attack me all at once. I couldn't tell the girl that we were in *Maximum Overdrive*, she'd flip out.

She tried to get me to come in her bus but I thought she was a giant pumpkin creature posing as a young girl trying to lure me inside to eat me. While she hid in the bus from the heat I kept having visions of the Tarot Joker crucified and staked onto the Satanic Symbol of sulphur – the double cross of the Leviathan. I too would be nailed to it in due.

In order to fool the intergalactic TV channels, I enacted the end of *Who Framed Roger Rabbit* where Bob Hoskins is punching himself in the face and doing prat falls to make the Weasels laugh themselves to death. There I was, throwing my body into the air and lashing into the dirt, getting up and punching myself, kicking myself like I was Shawn Micheals overselling in a wrestling match to an opponent of myself.

When I was sure that I had saved the human race, I crawled into the bus where we watched more Pro Wrestling. I was Vince McMahon on screen, the savior of the human race who had traveled 10,000 years into the future. Yet I was watching myself on Earth.

We watched *3rd Rock From The Sun*. Messages that my mother had assumed different forms because she was an alien from another galaxy and was acting as a background character on multiple sitcoms unveiled to me. Because Earth had really been destroyed by aliens the night *Independence Day* came out in 1996. That Friday night premiere they had launched their attack to coincide with the movie, as a bad in joke with the aliens.

For whatever reason I was still alive though and I needed to join the intergalactic sting operation. My mother – in the form of this girl I was once in love with – was standing atop the bridge in the distance where the flashing red light and large American flag was. I had to climb to the top of it to meet up and save the human race from the coming alien assault (which had already happened 20 years prior).

I think I told my friend that I would marry her, then I left the bus and went for a walk into the night. Everything became dark & deranged. I missed the meeting on the bridge because I couldn't figure out how to get up there. The window of opportunity to defeat the aliens had passed, and I screwed everyone because my inaction. Oopsie, I'll just slip away. Like Bart Simpson – *"It was like that when I got here."*

Somehow I walked all the way downtown and ended up on the waterfront in a section unfamiliar to me. I had visions that I was at war with another powerful Magickian who was using Qliphotic powers against my Tree Of Life powers. I had wild visions of being able to enter the different Sephirot spheres and become one with the color & divine emanation they represent. I was bouncing around The Tree Of Life comparing it to the ornament bulbs of a Christmas tree. I was able to move the colors to different Sephirot and change the entire power structure of my internal dimensions.

I returned to camp – I was now Tarot Joker and she was Harley. She clearly knew I was insane, as I was talking about how my father was an astrophysicist and how she was the smartest person on Earth because she knew how the color scale worked.

I wandered off again. The beer distillery down the street was somehow a holding tank of the souls of people on Earth who were turned into jelly creatures during the alien invasion & were being used like sex slaves – an intergalactic Epstein Island inside the containment unit in the distillery basement. Just like in *Ghostbusters*.

I sat on the corner knowing I was part of the sting operation against this sex crime palace. I was waiting for my orders from my father who was a cop from another world. All the cars that began passing me – I could differentiate if they were on my side or the side of the aliens by what colors they were painted with. All the cops were coming to save the day – and I would form their parade.

I started walking to the main road – fire hydrants & signs were half-human, half-metal hybrids just kind of hanging out, like merged people when they describe the aftermath of the Philadelphia Experiment with people stuck in walls. I started to lead this parade of ghost cars down the street – *"that's right aliens, were coming for you."* I was walking by businesses, knocking on their glass, giving them the raised fist salute.

Eventually all the cops vanished. The aliens had won. I was alone in a hostile world abandoned by my plot. I was the Tarot Joker again, and this was my new Gotham. I crawled in my tent and soon fell asleep.

The next morning I had visions that Christopher Nolan – his soul was trapped in Bane's breathing apparatus & constantly tortured as if in Hell. Bane was a demonic creature huffing on the torment of Nolan, and the opening sequence in *Dark Knight Rises* with the plane – the body Bane leaves in the wreckage was really David S. Goyer (*another threat from the Infernal Forces blatantly ruling Hollywood).

Wake up my friend – we watch *3rd Rock From The Sun*. Someone called her – I heard the voice mention my dead brother. *He was alive!* Secretly an intergalactic cop! I had to go to the bakery to facilitate a handoff of an alien child of a space dignitary who was kidnapped by space pirates. At the coffee shop I watched the deal go down in full.

Relieved, I walked to the school next door and plopped down on the playground bench. There was a black guy with his son playing catch. I thought the ball was the soul of the kidnapper now caught, and they were playing catch with the Black & White Diamond of The Tree Of Life and Tree Of Death. The man nodded to me – he <u>was</u> me. He was me as a cop in reality and I was in the simulation and I was a computer program who helped free his son. And now I was able to watch them play ball together.

I went back to the coffee shop and found a receipt on the ground – the numbers I had to punch into the toilet at a grocery store a mile away and then my portal to the world I came from would open. I walked 2 miles there and it didn't work. I knew I was stranded.

On the train ride home all my murdered friends from Occupy were on The Max, all with blackened, burned skin. They were paying me respects as the last one left one who could avenge them. See, my friend at camp was the alien queen who had them all killed. It was up to me to continue surveillance against her.

Back to camp where eventually two other people had come over, plus my friend. She wanted me to get in her U-Haul truck but I thought once the door closed I'd be trapped in Hell for 10,000 years. So I just walked away, escaping them.

I kept walking & walking. Everywhere I went people merged with fire hydrants & cars – ghosts coming out of the walls, hallucinations of people mocking me, stalking me like they were going to cause great bodily harm. The more I walked the more I realized aliens had won & anyone left was a robot. All cars were being driven by robots.

I hid down a darkened street where I knew I was being followed because my phone. I acted out a dramatic play for the screen to throw off my pursuers, then I destroyed my cell by stomping it into the cement. I kept walking & walking. All the people were mocking me – the ravens, the crows. I was in a place like the movie *Dark City* waiting for the terrain to flip to The Sun. But when it did it would create a worldwide hydrogen explosion and everyone would die.

I was the Mayor of Portland but I had been framed as a Ted Bundy serial killer in a conspiracy by another mayor trying to take my place. At camp the girl was nowhere to be found and had left an angry note on my tent because her tooth was hurting. I was supposed to take her to the hospital. I felt horrible.

This local guy who used to drive her to return bottles showed up and chastised me – he'd taken her to the hospital that night. I began apologizing because all my Tree Of Life colors were out of place. I thought he was an angel from God and that the heavens were reprimanding me for misplacing my Divine Emanations with incorrect color coding.

I started blubbering in front of this man. Telling him I was on the autistic end, I was a little slow. He wandered off silently, feeling bad for me while not understanding I had no clue what was happening.

Waited for the girl to come back but she was freaked out by me. I was telling her I was waiting for her – I wasn't sure if it was her though. I was stopping her from entering her own vehicle because I thought she might be a clone. She finally realized I was having some kind of legitimate schizophrenic break. She hid in her car, unsure of how to proceed.

I took a walk, and I slowly morphed into Dr. Johnathan Crane – The Scarecrow from the Batman comics. She found me wandering around the lot in my stupor and led me to my tent – that it was a safe zone & nothing could go wrong. Static & emotionless, I sat down in the tent thinking my straw brimmed Scarecrow hat was atop my head. Within the perimeters of a 6 foot by 6 foot plastic tent the fear swelled up every contour of space.

We must examine how thoroughly traumatic, terrifying & far reaching this abrupt change into Scarecrow was. If you are unfamiliar with *Batman*, Crane is the ultimate Archetype of Fear and in terms of Magick encapsulates Fear Magick.

What of the use of fear in Magickal practice? Raw terror is a tool that can be utilized on many fronts – shock & awe campaigns to inflict maximum psychological damage. There are many avenues to explore fear and all its omnidirectional uses. Many Supervillains have relied upon fear – it's part of the hustle, no doubt.

But let us examine The Fear King – Dr. Crane. As you may tell, his signature gimmick is fear. And his choice of weapon is his fear toxin manufactured into gas which he himself created as a mad chemist. At first he was a deranged psychologist experimenting with fear spurned to revenge from his lifetime bullying. They had beat him up and called him Scarecrow his entire life because he was thin & lanky. Thus he donned the costume.

However, you must understand that Scarecrow doesn't actually become The Scarecrow until he starts dosing himself with his own fear toxin and enjoying it. He becomes a junkie for his own chemically induced terror. He permanently lives in this bad trip world of his own creation, on purpose. And this is why Scarecrow is scary. He is a living archetype of terror. He might not be physically imposing, but his mind is wildfire.

This leads us to the core of Black Magick – specifically psychic attacks of Baneful Magick. The thing that all these Left Hand Path practitioners often forget – for Black Magick to work it needs a psychologically vulnerable target. Quite simply, Black Magick *feeds on fear*. If your target is unafraid of you – if you simply have no hook into their minds – then it will likely be rendered moot.

Now Witches generally know what's up – to be effective, these types of psychic Black Magick attacks are known throughout the spellcasting Witchy underground as a technique best described as the "Voodoo Vice." As in a voodoo doll or poppet squeezed into a mechanical vice. Every day you twist it a little tighter, the doll crushes more & more until eventually the pressure makes the stuffing pop out.

In other words, you find all kinds of creative ways to apply psychological pressure – you slowly f**k with someone's mind and you slowly drive them insane. Fear is like a forcefield that surrounds our being. Pulling these strings can be a wild spectacle.

The path of Fear Magick is not for the weak of mind or faint of heart. You have to build up your tolerance of fear in order to wield it properly. You have to work on the limits of your own fear. You must confront and master it all. Once nothing shakes or rattles you anymore, then you tolerance is way up. And trust me, if you are to be a Supervillain who wheels & deals in fear, you best be unafraid.

Furthermore, manipulating your own fear is both conscious work and shadow work at once. Fear has its own shadow within the larger shadow, dig? So learn not to be haunted by fear, but to instead haunt fear itself. That is the mark of a true Supervillain.

Anyway, there I was – fear turned alive. Yet somehow, despite being a Black Hole, I fell asleep. When my mind came into focus I had visions of The Tree Of Life but in the context of a puzzle book I got from my grandparents when I was 11. I saw the entire Tree and all its living parts come alive as if a cartoon. Elevation by elevation it unfurled its majesty to me. I knew I had reached The Wheel of Fortune. Everything else was like watching a pinball game – like a Vegas game with bells & whistles flashing.

My father – the one from the intergalactic sting operation against the Epstein Distillery – was now outside my tent, leaned against the car and crying. He wanted so bad to make contact with me and I with him, but it would break all the space laws.

He vanished and then I knew if I left my tent all my possessions would change to an alternate dimension version of them and it would again be 10,000 years in the future. But I did have to go pee, and afterwards began following people on the street for their clothing colors like I was cars the prior night.

My tent was a kiln and I had to sacrifice myself to it in order to set people free. I stripped naked and went into my tent and laid down to die and be like a voodoo doll of clay turned into some melted object.

I got dressed, left the tent & saw a U-Haul truck honking as it drove by. I knew it was all the jelly creatures from the Epstein containment unit being set free. I looked to the sky and saw them all cheering me, little bright lights like stars in the clear blue sky.

Immediately I became The Fool in the Gringonneur Tarot. Little children in red were before me, and I held their hands walking them through the parking lot. As denizens of this New Eden on Earth I had to teach them how to restart civilization.

I began shouting at the sky the books that would be needed to restart from scratch. Suddenly the most important tomes overtook me – the Ninja. Like an incantation hollered at the Gods, I dramatically waved my arms upwards and proclaimed: *"Stephen K. Hayes!"* Suddenly a murder of crows burst from the pine tree as if they heard my command and flew in all directions carrying the info of the Ninja to the humans left in this barren land. Because it had all been abandoned, save for some stragglers.

I laid down on the ground and saw a plane go by overhead. It was carrying the alien queen that I saved from the Epstein Containment Unit. A booming voice said: *"You just sacrificed yourself here to let the girl go – what a big pair of balls you have."*

Suddenly, in real life, some kid walked up to me in the parking lot and said something intelligible. He pulled scissors from his pocket & dropped them to the ground & walked away. I took it as a message from The Simulation like, *"There you go asshole, that's what I think of your big balls. You still belong to us, and we're cutting them off. F**k you."*

I laughed at his threat to neuter me and left the scissors on the ground. To this day I still have no idea who that kid was or what was going on there. Regardless, as I lay on the ground I had visions of The Fool Trump and that I was The Fool. I was protected because I gave up fighting and reverted back to zero, the number of omnidirectional potential.

I was again Tarot Joker laying on the ground in a protective circle of my own mind that was the zero. As long as you were in the confines of the zero, no one could hurt you. You were master of the world. You just had to give up fighting first. You sacrificed all control and became The Golem of God.

Laughing constantly, The Fool lay in his zero and watched the clouds change shape. All the faces in the clouds were smiling, all on his side for once. He remembered the 3 Magic Words of Judaism and that these were the command prompts for the simulation he was now trapped in. *"Aleph!"* he declared, raising his hand to the sky. A huge cloud formed. The more he said Aleph, the more he controlled air and the clouds.

The other words – Shin and Mem for Water & Fire respectively – he did not dare to utter. He did not know the Noah's Ark like deluge that would be created or the fire apocalypse that may be rendered from uttering the Holy Words.

I had a vision of 4 women I knew as Watchtowers of their Magickal Coven. Though none of these women hung out, I realized they were my sloppy Witchcraft Coven and that united we created the perfect 5 pointed Pentagram. The girl I stayed with, the two sex workers I'd met years ago, and the zany Clown Stripper who at times would appear.

One of the sex workers – the girl with the Lilith tattoo – she was wearing a full red body suit. She was also a simulation and created for me as a companion inside this simulation. In the normal world I ignored her but it turns out I just didn't understand her because although we were crested to be a unified program, we were given too different commands and she could never be in the same place as me at the same time.

I had mad visions of the Pentagram – sharp, bold, massive. I couldn't stop laughing. I'd been made Prince of this World. It started sprinkling a little, so I climbed in the U-Haul. I could smell & taste metal. Somehow the goth sex workers had been turned into the wrenches & bear mace cans & screwdrivers & power tools in the back of the truck.

They informed me that the Epstein Distillery had been turned into a queer goth sex club, like a giant bathhouse, and that they were all going. I was having too much fun where I was though, and wished them to have a good evening. I sat down like Charles Manson stroking his beard & picked up an acoustic guitar. Behind me, the wrenches & screwdrivers were all f**king in an orgy.

Hallucinating, I saw a crowd of young people from barren Earth approach the back of the U-Haul, as if I was a demagogue about to speak. I hopped up and gave them a speech for the ages, telling them they had reached the rebirth of the human race.

"Begone!" – they all disappeared and he was in another dimension, this time of Djinn made of the spark that detonated the Hydrogen Bomb. I could smell & taste metal even heavier; I was a being made of atomic material birthing a whole different life form apart from Carbon based organisms.

It began storming heavily – water just poured down. Had I said Mem by accident? The pine tree was shriveled up & weeping. I began tearing up and rushed to it's defense. I hugged the tree passionately to bolster its sad feelings. I felt the pine sap slather over me while I cushioned its nervous breakdown.

Soaked and loving it, I crawled into the bus. Things had quickly changed – the townspeople knew I was a Witch and that I must be destroyed. They were coming for me with pitchforks & torches. Their plan was to take me, my friend and the cat & fuse us all together as a statue to be burned in the public square at midnight.

Just then the girl pulled back up. She had a guy with her to make sure I would get where I was going. She was frantic: "*We need to get you to the hospital immediately – you need to come with me.*" I hopped out of the bus totally confused, crying, because the townspeople would get us unless we moved fast. I was in my socks and dragging my backpack filled with all my best Magick books. I couldn't let the townspeople know the powers of Magick, lest it ruin the world from the budding knowledge.

She got me in the car & we were off. I kept asking what year it was. I was again the Mayor being set up as Ted Bundy. She was a part of the police force secretly on my side and working against the plot; she was taking me where could hide like a safe house. I was to be the prize witness in whatever legal situation would arise.

We got to the psych ward in short time. The blocky colored plastic chairs were colors just like the cars I was following around days ago. I knew I was in luck. I didn't understand it, but I was sloppily checking myself in. I signed on the dotted line what I thought were legal documents for the court case.

They led me to an area with a rubber room. They told me I had to get changed immediately, they would take my wallet, my clothes, my belongings, everything. I just had to put on the green scrubs and enter the rubber room of my own accord.

But I hung halfway in the door blubbering. I kept telling them I'm not Ted Bundy. The nurses kept saying my name – first and last, first and last. Making me feel like a split personality person they were trying to catch on video.

Eventually, after standing there blubbering thinking I was about to be executed or pushed into Hell to be tortured in the room, a security guard just came up, threw me down, held me down, and injected me with who knows what in my butt cheek with a hypodermic needle. I completed putting on the green scrubs, but I was getting tired fast.

All I remember is something about looking in a plastic mirror on the wall of a bathroom (*there must have been a toilet attached*) and in my reflection I saw the girl, the cat and myself all fused together being tortured as one mutant creation. I staggered back towards the rubber room and it's matted floor and THUMP zzzzzzzzzzzzzzz...

Adventures In The Psych Ward

Madness is embarrassing. It ruins your life but also makes you look like a total fool beyond comparison. It is what it is. You were fried from psychedelics & schizoid tendencies long ago. Your brain has been crushed in a mechanical vice of Manic Depressive bipolar nightmare your entire life. It fused with the years long exhaustion of a Global Pandemic. Finally, it went POP. Everything came back all at once, with plenty of new territory to oblige.

In all this Kabbalistic literature, there is this reoccurring thing called "The Vision Of The Throne of God." And all of these ecstatic spiritual experiences that are supposed to be brought on when you truly receive. This whole conduit, Gods pure channel Atzilut opens up to you & you get engulfed – it becomes this luminous experience.

I do remember at one point one of the Doctors jumped out and asked, "*Are you having a religious experience?*" while I was drifting along the labyrinth not talking. They were trying to figure it out because I was completely silent the whole time. And whenever I did talk it was some babble that they could only get fragments out of, none of which made any sense. I needed to hide everything.

It's a long story to even explain the perimeters of. Basically I walked into a totally natural bad acid trip combined with the remnants of real bad acid trips & whatever other mind poisons I had ingested over my lifetime. This led to a new conspiracy against me or involving me that changed every 5 minutes – often world endangering & crucial to be solved for the sake of all humanity.

Other times, it was assassination attempts against me, threats of murder, being framed for something I had no part of – being part of secret plots against mayors or an asset to an intergalactic sting operation. The aliens were up to wild shit – some of them on my side, others hostile.

Mania had finally arrived in my life to the point where it so enveloped my entire being that it was like blasting off in a rocket ship. Once I hit a certain point all of the hallucinations took over and I went totally schizophrenic. It was a slow burn process, with the imagined ghost of Heath Ledger creeping up on me as the gunshot of a marathon.

I never had mania take over my life so completely – my body, mind, spirit & every vibrational level. It went soaring & I lost all control. And this coincided with me breaking through mentally to the realms of Magick and the subtleties of energy and all these mystic Alchemical experiences. Plus everything the Tarot Cards taught, everything Golden Dawn was preaching – The Zohar, The Tree Of Life – the extreme enthusiasm & faith & wonder & propulsion I had for it intermingled with extreme mania and lapsed into delusional psychosis.

This was all rising to a crescendo out of my control – it just went off. As it progressed, I understood less & less who I was. And I was lost in a complete dream world filled with electricity.

Somehow I walked into an upside down Tarot Pack and I was now The Fool leading everyone off the cliff like lemmings only to drop straight into my bizarre *Alice In Wonderland* fantasy world based on all the decks I'd ever seen. Everyone was now liable to become an image from The Cards, all of them entrapped in the web of my Alchemical Great Work. All were motifs in Medieval paintings...

There I was, mute in a padded cell. I don't know how much time had passed, but I was awake now & they'd pushed a plate of food in the room. I was back in *The Dark Knight* being shown a separate movie. Now my brain was replaying the hospital explosion sequence.

Joker was really my mother who was really Lilith who was really Poison Ivy and all were combined as The Joker on the school bus escaping the explosion even though Clayface was really Joker the entire movie except for this specific scene.

The red incision mark on the stomach of Joker's henchman when he sewed the cell phones in him – the cellphone colors were the Sephirot of The Tree, the red sewn gash was the Red Snake of Lilith. Lilith was everywhere, and so was Samael, who was really Two-Face. I was Clayface now, a Golem in that rubber room awaiting Two Face / Samael to come carve my face into a clown.

The orderlies kept coming in trying to talk to me. They had to wait for some form of response before taking me to the room where they dump in all the crazies. I had yet to reach that state of security for them.

The lead Doctor, this imposing man, kept coming in and trying to talk me out. I must have been in this rubber room for nearly 2 days. I cannot remember how many times they entered or left, but there must have been at least 4 meals.

Eventually the imposing Doctor came in again and just plainly told me he was The Duke and that there were no Monsters. I knew he was on my side then – I had to tell him the secret password. It came cautiously out of my throat, weak & childlike: "*Dok-tor Zee-ro.*" He shook my hand, pulled me up & began walking me down corridors where methed out crazies were watching TV's in hypnotic trances, rocking back & forth.

I was led to the room where they dump them all in, a large holding tank lined with Lazyboy recliners and gym mat's on the floor so you could sleep. I was with at least 50 other maniacs, psychotics, delulu folks & schizophrenic breaks. It must have been a Saturday night, and it was bustling.

Outside there was a Trailblazers basketball game letting out (we were next to Moda Center) – tons of loud people outside. It sounded like a war was going on. I thought the Aliens were waging battle like *War of the Worlds*. The extraterrestrials had gotten us. Everyone knew about The Takeover and we were segregated from the resistance fighters.

There was no bother talking about it to the other patients, because the microphones were listening. We all just knew & nodded at each other. Like me, everyone else had just given up. We were all waiting for the next step. Maybe other humans would come rescue us? Perhaps they would break through the Cosmic defenses of The Invaders? And then we'd take the fight to the streets.

We all watched *Return of The Jedi* on TV. The aliens began handing out pills. If you eat them, you deteriorate. You turn to sand and all the water melts out of you, and you are pool of liquid on the floor. I fake taking my meds & throw them in the trash – ain't gettin' me Lizard Person! Fall asleep on a mat on the floor...

Next day, wake up to blonde kid with a shaved head, maybe 22. I think it's Infomercial Satan Guy in another body and we're both trapped here together. He talks how we're all doomed and never getting out.

Across the room there is a Space Queen from a far flung Galaxy where the planet is completely modeled after Viking Mythology – they call her the Norse Queen of the Ice Planet. I know she's being held captive, and for whatever reason the Intergalactic Police – as a form of punishment – are going to fuse her & him together as one hermaphrodite being. This was the judgment of the High Intergalactic Supreme Court.

The kid starts talking about how he wants to be my brother, and that we were going to hang out in the parking lot drinking beers & smoking weed. I envision the little parking lot I was trapped in Summer of 2020 during Covid, outside the gas station by my old rehearsal space. I was back in Covid world now and it was raging once again and there was no vaccine, but now it was a virus supplanted by the aliens to slowly destroy our world & prime it for the inevitable takeover.

The kid gets really aggressive and starts shouting at the orderlies: *"You people are criminals! Criminals!!"* They drag him off into another room as he struggles against them, surely to be fused to the Norse Queen. I never see him again.

I look around and I know we're in a holding facility on Jupiter. 10,000 years have gone by since I was captured. Orderly comes up. Ask if he's ever since *John Carpenter's They Live*. Says, *"Yeah I love that movie."* Then, openly – being like, *"That's right – f**k you alien – you didn't kill me and it's the deep future now"* – I tell him I'm 10,000 years old. And I'm like thinking, *"Now what, bitch?"*

He goes and tells someone what I said and another orderly rushes over and takes my pulse. They make me eat pills. They are treating me different now. At first they must have thought I was blasted on tweak or acid, but now they realized I was sober and had no medical history for this sort of thing. They must have contacted my relatives, which I can't process but is nevertheless not a good thing because all it will sow is panic.

Plus I simply can't deal with my mother or stepfather right now. To be honest I don't even know they exist, let alone anyone else. The only person I can think of from my life is the girl who checked me in, and I think she's in another ward somewhere experiencing some other adventure. I have also completely forgotten about cigarettes.

Time goes on. A guy hops like a bunny on the floor as doctors follow him around with clipboards & pens. They wheel in a tank I think is filled with an extraterrestrial forced to become liquid – the daughter of a space dignitary / the alien queen I thought my friend had become days ago. She was turned into water and had to be dumped into the toilet and flushed through a special system so they would reunite her body drop by drop.

And whatever was really happening, there was a young girl under there crying, begging for her mother, begging to go home. I think she may have ate poison and they were trying to force her to puke. Either way I think I'm the one who ratted her out to the space authorities. My hands are clean of this judgment.

Bunny Guy gets into a debate with me about Jesus. I immediately say he sucks – the dude is taken aback. He explains, "Well it's not about actually being the son of God – it's about having a positive example of humane actions." Something lit up my brain – it just connected to all this Catholic stuff that was forced on me. I knew the Bible better then most and I could answer questions honestly and responsibly about the subject. I wasn't preaching, I was simply a database.

It is the moment that started the whole weird thing of me becoming a religious icon to the other patients. Because I became a dispenser of the message of Jesus – not because I believed in it, but because I knew it very well and people wanted to ask questions. They thought they were approaching a holy wise man but I'm just sitting there like the computer that spits out 42 in *Hitchhikers Guide*. I was an open book of The Gospel.

Myself & Bunny Guy – we talk magnetic polarity. So we communicate our polarities in unison, structuring the energy fields around us, moving around & changing position by mimicking each others movements like the mirror scene in that Marx Bros movie.

He tells me the orderlies are all robots – you can say whatever you want to them, they won't reply. And if you ask for anything they just give it to you. He shows me how to get free coffee & nicotine gum. The robots of the aliens are our slaves! *We win!* Then he went back to hopping around and I fell asleep.

Next day I wake up – *Hunt For Red October* is on TV. I climb into the Lazy Boy recliner facing the screen but soon the channel changes to *Face / Off* with Nick Cage. And I realize I have the remote control. As I'm clicking through the channels, the cushioned chair become The Throne Of God and I am subjected to "The Vision."

As I flip through channels, the commercials and the color schemes become direct messages from the highest channel of God. Everything I'm viewing is upgrading me with every surfed channel and advertisement – like *ker-chunk*, *ker-chunk*, this Alchemical process soaring.

I keep seeing numbers on screen, like how to order things from infomercials. There is a portable landline phone next to me and I start dialing the numbers, confirming how I want to upgrade. It is the magnified perception of Atzilut light which acquiesces through weird bleeps & bloops.

I get to certain point and the radiance is too blinding. I have become a new Spiritual Being entirely, all in the span of 10 minutes. Like a Game Show where a contestant is given 10 minutes to wildly collect prizes before the special clock halts, God's window of upgrade opportunity simply dissipated. I was on Jupiter again in an alien holding cell.

I realize my friend is in a separate facility and think she's being tortured – I must somehow get her number. I shake the portable phone in my hand, frustrated and broken that I am condemned to her suffering. I began freaking out and crying from ineptitude.

This female mental patient with long brown hair pops up before me. Tells me it will be OK. She's not supposed to have contact but she gives me a hug anyway. She is up to serious business that day. She's like the Roman God Mercury between all the screwjobs, passing along information and helping different people. She's the go-to between all these little clusters of people all staying to themselves.

More drugs from the staff, more pools of people. Later at night this younger kid, maybe 20, gets admitted. He's all doped up on pills, talking about how his grandmother just died from Covid and his other friend committed suicide and he's so god damn tired. I ask him to play Batman. Who is his favorite character? Robin! *This was Robin!*

Now everyone in the ward had to play Batman too. I began circling the ward asking the other crazies which characters they wanted to be for this game. I wasn't going to be Joker though, that could be some other guy. This time I was The Mad Hatter.

From this moment onward, I was having a total blast. I was never more happy then I ever was in my entire life. I was where I was always meant to be – *I was finally in Arkham!* I felt like I was 10 again, at the top of my game.

The new Scarecrow sat at the desk with a pile of papers the brown haired girl acquired from the other psych ward patients. He was pensively studying them all. This guy, black guy with green hair – he was now Johnathan Crane. I kept shouting: *"Go Crane! Do it – do it!"* He never looked up. The brown haired girl kept whispering secret things in his ear.

Suddenly the psych ward was a spaceship that stopped working, and we were stuck floating through space. Unless we got the engines working again we'd perish. The only way to do this? I had to immediately put all my Qaballistic knowledge to test – I had to draw out the entire Tree Of Life with its appropriate colors and write how it all works in abbreviated code form. The AI running the spaceship had lost this data & it was crucial for it's reboot.

I felt The Eyes Of God behind my shoulder, as if this were my final test before a doctorate diploma. God had to know that someone in Portland still understood how to do this. This was the entire point of why I was being shown everything I have. It wasn't only the spaceship at stake, but PDX would be swallowed up into the Earth with a quake had not one person be there to defend it. I was the last believer.

I spent an hour on this schematic, perfectly arranged & brightly colored. Gave it to Scarecrow. The brown haired girl looked up at me with an insane smile and began nodding her head. I stood up like a champion and waved my hands in the air: *"Mem, Shin, ALEPH!"*

The engines began again, the entire psych ward rumbled. *We were saved!* I sat back down, and I was fully the Tarot Joker. Everyone was now a scene depicted in The Golden Tarot of The Renaissance...

Next thing I remember is waking up on a medical table with a woman taking my blood. She realizes I'm awake, has startled eyes. I let her know not to be afraid. I say, childishly: *"Skibble dee bibble dee bop."* She starts laughing,

Doctors come in – "*Do you want to be transferred to Unity East?*" I think it's part of the conspiracy – but which one? Not sure, but I'm supposed to.

I'm introduced to my own room with a roommate, and soon we are talking Jesus. I respond honestly, remembering the conversation with Bunny Guy. I'm not a Christian obviously – I'm Dr. Zeero, the Magickal Supervillain – but I can answer honest questions about the whole deal since I was raised by a Catholic family.

Soon a watery Ted Bundy began emerging from the toilet. I shout him down reading Revelations. Grow hoarse, can't do it anymore – one of these Bundy's gets away to cause mayhem down the hall. We're in trouble – blood will be on my hands.

"*Keep it quiet!*" shouts the orderly. They think I'm a religious nut, so do all the other patients hearing this. I must have been very loud because it takes a lot of vocal force to shout down Ted Bundy back into H20 formlessness.

I go out to the darkened rec room. The Orderly – I think it's my friend from high school, that it's a sleepover at his house. He gets me a hot chocolate. Forget why, but I start getting agitated & loud. They had zero tolerance for my antics; they must have marked me as a potentially violent patient. Immediately I was jumped by 3 security guys, big black guys, and injected with something in the ass cheek and thrown in rubber room. Zzzzzzzzzzzzzz....

"*How did you get into Michael's room last night?*" The doctors are confused, and I have no ideas what they are talking about. I can't even remember what happened from the rubber room until now. Another day, apparently. This is when the days really become chunks of memories. I don't know what was when or what day or how long...

But I remember eating food off trays & coloring books in the rec room. My roommate had a deck of playing cards. I was trying to help him figure it all out. That somehow there was serendipitous connections.

I began laying down card by card on the table – each one was a person I knew in high school, and I arranged them on the table as if it were everyone's houses on the map of the terrain I used to ride my bike around. The scheme of my teenage days & friends – all were vaguely familiar to him. We were getting to the bottom of a Great Mystery...

The next day my roommate left – I had snapped him out of it, apparently. I had got him to call someone from a note in his pocket who then talked him back to reality. They picked him up & he was gone. Onto the next...

Things are quite fuzzy, but I had become a religious figure to the other patients. Big beard with intense Jesus answers, one by one they would approach me with Jesus trivia. I have become a Prophet to them. Furthermore, someone wrote "Captain Kirk" on my door. The healthcare workers had begun calling me this – I was default running the ship.

We need to talk about how we were now in a sub-level simulation that God created, and that God was sending himself down a tube of fire and incinerating himself with 3000 years of burning alive to reach me once every 12 years. I was the secret Jesus Christ and his son, but because he created me as an AI bot this was also his digital simulation. He was secretly working as a staff member of the psych ward yet changing his appearance constantly so I never knew which one. He was a background lurker.

Next chunk – at night, watching TV. I try to escape & the guard stops me at the door, like a silent stone statue that came alive and clunked over to block me. I retreat to the couch. On Netflix is a show about a girl from India, 19, soon to be married. I'm given two option, one of which I must immediately choose – either I can turn into her and live the rest of her life or I can turn into a pumpkin creature in the name of God eating all the souls of the damned, like deleted data disposal unit in a computer program. I would be the enforcer of The Abyss on The Tree Of Life, such as Abaddon.

What would it be Dr. Zeero? Are you altering into a 19 year old chick from Bangladesh or are we going full on Pumpkin Monster? *Feed me!* exclaimed I, to God. And so I became The Soul Eater. And if you thought being The Scarecrow was a scary place to be, you don't know what it's like becoming a Halloween Pumpkin Creature that eats the souls of the damned, tasting like copper and rust.

To think that my life was destined for "T-Minus Pumpkin Creature" – it's the last place I ever thought reality would take me. Yet there I was, vines dripping from the top of my head, razor sharp teeth smiling jaggedly. Once I slipped into that manifestation I became stuck there for some time. I fell asleep and when I awoke, Pumpkin Monster I was still.

This vegetable creature now watched TV in the rec room. On the monitor was a special about the Menendez brothers. Guy rocking back & forth watching it, a Mexican kid – he was one of them and watching his crimes on TV. Soon he would be led out of the room and executed. They would be fed to me as dinner, the Pumpkin Beast. I watched him rock back & forth like a gigantic shrimp. He was the Leviathan but I was much worse – I would gobble up his whale-like body as if a shrimp.

They were led out by the orderlies and only I remained, drawing pumpkin creatures and coloring Witches with crayons. They soon brought me dinner on a plate. I devoured their essences in the name of God and burped a loud belch.

Next day there is this weird Russian guy wandering around with gnarly teeth. In one room a girl made of plastic is being operated on by demonic clowns...

Another day passes. At some point, Pumpkin Monster wore off. I was again whoever I was – a human for sure, even though I did not know my own name. Finally go outside to the little enclosed backyard court. Plants were like rubber. Some of us tossed around a football. I go inside and my friend had dropped off some clothes – one of which is a t-shirt with a Coroner patch from an actual morgue. Now the patients are really freaked by me – the bearded Jesus Prophet is now The Coroner.

I go in my room to change clothing and all the other patients go in their rooms and also change their clothes following my lead. Go back to the table, they all come out and sit down. I go change clothes again – they all go & change their clothes. We all go back to the table. They all want to know about God.

Two doctors interview me solo. I keep remembering Bunny Guy. They are asking serious questions though to which I cannot reply, as dictated by conspiracy. But I know they are robots. I slowly take a pen, stick it up my nose, then snot rocket it like space ship to the side and just smile back at them. Those androids won't ever figure me out.

Next day (maybe) there is a patient at the table, younger guy early 20's. His name is Baby Sam and I literally believe he is Samael the Angel. He tells me I'm getting out today. He shows me we have an iPad to listen to music and makes me listen to 3 Inches Of Blood. It's the first time I start to realize there are objects again. There are electronics. There are tangible things I can wrap my head around.

I get led to a physical therapy class where they are teaching stretches & meditation. They have me play some board game with a girl that had just attempted suicide. I think I'm at the Ypsilanti college in Michigan and I'm in my early 20's.

See Sam again – *"Can I get your number?"* I realize there are phone numbers. That there are... people I can call. I realize there is a Computer over there – Facebook? I remember that. Wait a minute – an acoustic guitar on the wall I can play? Start tuning the guitar, using my mind. Things start normalizing. By the time I put the guitar back on the wall, I started rapidly coming to.

All at once I returned – I realized where I was. Totally disoriented & all drugged out & fuzzy, of course, but I knew I was in a psych ward. Erratically to the nurse: *"They said I was leaving today."* *"Who said that?"* *"Well, Baby Sam."* *"Who?"* *"Wait, my old boss can figure it out..."*

The first person who popped into my head was my manager from this pizza place I was dishwasher of, right when Covid started. I went on the computer with dizzy eyes trying to get his number. I wanted to log into Facebook but couldn't remember my email or password.

Back to the doctor. *"How long until I'm out?"* Tells me, *"You're free to go whenever you like – you checked yourself in here."* I finally saw my opening for escape. Despite having a blast the whole time, reality was rapidly coming back and I was very aware that I was in a whole heap of trouble.

Now, the smart thing would be just to stop and start talking. Sort out what went on here with the doctors at hand. By no means did I want to leave or should have left – truth was I was having the time of my life. It's just that immediately the protester in me came to control the situation – *"Am I being detained? Am I free to go?"* I knew I was being recorded & monitored by the police, the state, the mental health establishment. So the answer was to get out immediately with no statement.

I demanded to leave and they just could not legally stop me. They soon got all my stuff, my backpack & clothing which were sealed in bags like evidence. I quickly got dressed as they were begging me to see a therapist and continue some kind of treatment.

They led me out of their labyrinth. As I was about to leave a detective with a notepad stood at that exit. I'd seen him before – from Occupy. He was the one watching all the protesters, not a hallucination or delusion – literally, was this dude building a case on me? They kept tabs on all of us, or was his job just dealing with the mentally ill? Was that why he was at the Occupy Camps in the first place?

He stood there excepting a statement with his little notepad. Instead, I just saluted him like a military officer and kept my mouth shut. Nodded, turned & bolted out the door as quick as I could, no shoes and in socks – right into early February where luckily it was 50 degrees and not snowing or raining...

In order for me to continue living with the girl she demanded that I get on the psych meds the doctors had prescribed. She absolutely was not going to deal with me otherwise. They put me on Haloperidol but it made me crazy. I could nor stop moving my legs all day and had to just keep walking & walking. It was miserable. I kept hallucinating rabbits & people.

I finally saw my regular doctor and his eyes bugged out as soon as he saw whatever was in the ward report. Immediately he put me on Abilify. Also, the telephone therapist had coerced me into being put on a watch list called the "vulnerable population" list, which would appear on cop computers, medical records, etc. It was a protective measure. I got roped into it without realizing what I was signing up for or agreeing to. I had marked myself.

The therapist called every few weeks & I told her the bare minimum. I worked on improving my relationship with the girl. But I knew I was fried and could be dangerous to her. I knew I had to go away.

I knew my life was over in many aspects. Can't tour again or be trusted to lead a band or simply be a musician in the ensemble. I'm nothing but a liability in a band, because music groups are like marrying several other people.

Can't travel Europe because they won't give more then a month supply of the drug. No matter what I say or do or how long its been, they think I'm a suicide risk. Can't play music 'cause my brain doesn't work as well anymore.

Understand that all these experiences were very real to me – I became The Pumpkin Monster, The Scarecrow, The Tarot Joker. These are all etched into my soul and now define the boundaries of where my mind has gone.

Can you understand the level of discipline needed to pull yourself back from this cataclysm? Can you understand how much effort & persistence & sheer bravery it takes not to unalive yourself when literally every machine in the world is about to kill you like in *Maximum Overdrive?* Or that you've been framed as a serial killer? Or that intergalactic sting operations are counting on you to solve interplanetary crimes? That the fate of the human race rests solely on your actions to solve a global crisis, yet you keep failing every single time, condemning The Earth?

I'm basically f**ked. One day I might wake up and not remember who anyone is anymore. That's my reality – I'm a dead man walking. Could become defensive in my schizoid state, do something crazy. You're a a time bomb potentially destructive & it makes you stay away from people.

So you are a walking nuclear warhead. Great. Will you lose it and try to drive a car or operate heavy machinery? Or you could think someone was against you and you have to defend yourself but you're just some deluded psycho about to attack an innocent person? This is the kind of reality you have to gamble with. Kiss your romantic life goodbye.

On that note know that I did everything I ever wanted to do in life. Things happened for me that never happened for other people, and a lot of the coolest things that ever happened occurred only because I got off my ass and used the willpower & imagination to launch all my epic, Magickal Adventures. I do not have regrets of this variety.

An outsider may remark that Magick drove me insane. As to my experience, I felt supercharged with an electricity I have never felt otherwise, just endlessly for days alongside visions that were ethereal and luminous. I stumbled into the peak of Merkabah Mysticism like the hand of YHVH came down from The Heavens and smooshed me in its grip. All at once, my mind saw with total clarity the infinite extent of The Great Work & I became a living Tarot pack…

And then, finally, it was time to get a Job…

We all know The Mask is wearing Me

When you practice Magick, you are liable to end up alone. And I don't mean not dating someone or having zero friends. When you completely invest yourself in Magick and make it part of your everyday life, you are always performing Magick because you are living it. It sets you apart from the vast mass of humanity.

It shouldn't, because it's an obvious idea to harness your willpower to the utmost extent – to learn self control & self mastery, then send those waves of energy & information into the world to cause change. This should not be that wild of a concept to people.

This path demands a strong mind to walk alone. The more elevated you become, the more alien you develop. The more fused to nature and your common man, the more isolated you come by default. It's quite the conundrum.

People just kind of become annoying to you. The fact that they aren't operating on your level – it becomes quite taxing when none are able to remotely consider the disciplines of mind power or spiritual alchemy.

The wiser you get the more you realize you are dealing with children – and Man-Children in America are endlessly manufactured. The just waste time playing video games & collecting toys until they are 40, ensnared with the mind of a 20 year old (or less).

Magick makes you hyper-aware of the children masquerading as adults. Likewise, the adults – those more responsible & self contained – are also gonna be way behind. You become, by proxy, the wizardly one they come to for advice or to learn these subjects or techniques. You may not be ready for this role. It is a strange situation 'cause there isn't anyone you can turn to.

Every path is unique and what works for you might not work for other people. No one is going to key up precisely, so there is loneliness. You become a lone wolf.

Magick is about constant growth and evolution – it's the pitfall of dramatically altering yourself and you don't know what you're going to end up like. To evolve is a gamble. It's gonna take your mind to places you never thought it could go.

Now understand I don't mean being "childlike" is bad, per se. One of the most important mindframes of Magick is to play as children play. Kids use their imaginations as the driving force of so many games & their overall perceptions. Go deeper in, don't refuse it.

Another subject – Brass Tax & Bottom Lines. When we talk about Chaos Magick or philosophies such as it, where you get to pick & choose & go paradigm hopping – there's a lot to consider. We're talking religion in general here as well. You must always ask yourself "what is the end result?" A) What is their vision of an afterlife and B) What is their concept of judgment? C) If you're going to buy into any of these religions what does that render your worldview into?

Similarly, we have to talk about Gods & Goddesses. All kinds of different Pagans   customize their own Pantheon to a scattershot of Daemons they think are cool. More often then not they haven't quite thought it through. Because when you're going to enter a very specific paradigm there's a whole history & cultural context for which it existed. You must absorb the mindframe of the consciousness that created all this stuff in order to Operate.

One example: Druidry – more about a structure and a notion then anything else. You have to understand the historical Druids weren't a religion, they were like overseers and they were like utilitarian priestly figures for Celtic culture as a whole.

There were many Deities among different tribes and The Druids basically were the priestly caste officiating over rituals. They didn't put their stamp of approval on any single religion. But they were definitely preachers of immortality and this was a Celtic thing. Their combined culture – there was this belief in an Otherworld that you would constantly be reincarnated from.

So with all that in mind, reincarnation is such a central thing to Celtic spirituality, their pantheist Pagan multi-God philosophy – Doc just doesn't think any of that's real. Doesn't believe in reincarnation from another world. So if you just don't believe in that, that is the brass tax bottom line deal.

Just like with Jesus Christ – there's a Hell that you go to and get tortured in if you don't follow scripture. And if you don't believe that is real then it makes your entire view crumble to ruin.

Doc bases his approach on extreme bottom lines. No "Otherworld" so that negates the entire Celtic pantheon. I like the idea of their Gods, I think they make rad mythological figures & symbols, they are gee-whiz neato representations of forces of nature or psychologies – but to truly ritualize & gain gnosis? You must buy into this Otherworld.

Doc doesn't believe in the Gods as if entities that you can communicate with from an invisible realm. Doc might buy into ghosts, spirits, some kind of invisible creature – but just because something says its Thoth doesn't make it so. These things would be vampiric psychic leeches by nature. Can't trust them, if they do indeed exist. That's why I say avoid all this Infernal Divine spirit conjuring jibber jabber – it just begs for trouble.

Furthermore, I'm perplexed by the Hindu Gods and cannot take them serious outside of being cool poster art. Except that one time I god juiced with Fudo Myoo. So, yeah, I did get some wild results poking around at something associated with Hinduism – but it was also a God that was absorbed into Hinduism and mutually picked up by Esoteric Buddhists, becoming the Ninja God. Fudo was hardcore, let me tell you.

I don't believe in Viking religion. The runes are fun but they are just fixed sigils that mean a handful of things – child's play, nothing more. And sigils – once again another prop to make your mind focus and release psychic energy.

Props are important, but learn to just flick it on. The Brass Tax & Bottom Line of Witchcraft is that it's a nature religion. Nature is about what's in front of you & merging with it fanatically. You know, just eat a bunch of magic mushrooms and wander off into that forest butt naked under a full moon & howl like the wolf & let it all out. That's what Witchcraft is truly about – all the High Magick stuff is the add on.

I'm pro-Wicca but I don't believe in the 3 Fold Law, no karma, none of this stuff. I don't believe in the Buddha and I don't think he was all that wise. All this wisdom is attached to him but it's again in the context of worldview. Buddha is selling all sorts of nonsense about the afterlife & reincarnation. I disagree with half the things he says.

I think the Dalai Lama is a joke – he was abducted as a child, brainwashed that he was a resurrected ex lama Magician guy and forced against his will to be the leader of his people. What is this other then a sick tale of child abuse? The whole thing is horribly wrong & tragic. *They kidnapped a child & forced him to run a cult!*

I want to meet the Dalai Lama and somehow give him whatever "Rosebud" would be, like in *Citizen Kane*. I shall snap him out of it. I wanna be the one that frees the Dalai Lama from the cult that absorbed him. Together we will make our escape. I just gotta get around Stephen K. Hayes somehow, 'cause that's one fierce bodyguard.

Anyway, the whole central premise in Buddhism – "*Buddha was so enlightened, oh the ever-flowing wisdom...*" Well he doesn't have a hedonist streak in him, doesn't know how to party, so why should I listen to him at all? If he can't foxtrot or boogie, what use is he?

Witchcraft is about merging with The Universe and Buddhism is all about escaping it for Nirvana, where you lose everything that makes you human. That's no fun. Where's the comedy? Where are the Comic Books? When is Halloween?

As far as Voodoo goes, I barely know anything about it, but I can say I'm highly skeptical of The Loa and anything called a "Saint." Again, what is the end result worldview? I'm a man of science & reason & logic. Does not compute; does not resonate.

And this hoodoo shit – it's ridiculous. It's Jesus Christ centered folkloric Witchcraft mixed with voodoo. I think. Isn't that basically whats up? But if you're gonna say Jesus is real, how can you support Witchcraft?

When you jump on social media it sets you up. You become someone who can be openly attacked or ridiculed or brought into the discussion of other people on different platforms. By virtue of just stepping up and going on the podium you set yourself up to be criticized. You can easily be an object of attack for trolls, hecklers, agitators & Keyboard Commandos of all stripes & varieties. So it's important people attack Dr. Zeero for the right reasons.

Understand that Doc here isn't necessarily at war with people on a personal level, but that Xiron is at war with certain ideas. So we got to talk about Dr. Zeero versus the Army of Darkness. And, uh, that's a big ol' field to cover.

Doc here sets apart from other Magickal people because my whole approach centers on Mind Power. I have differing ideas about certain things getting in the way of Mind Power or diluting it. Now this isn't to say that Zeero Xiron is a perfect person – Doc smokes weed, Doc likes to drink a little bit, party a little. He's not the ultimate in discipline, right? But there's no slack in my act and I'm disciplined mentally in the important ways.

As I've stated, I think the Gods & Goddesses are Avatars of psychology which you can concentrate on & fuse with & glean all kinds of interesting information. But then there are also The Dark Daemons – the Demonic, as well. Some are straight up Infernal, others have aspects of what we would call demonic. In regard to demons as the inhumane & volatile aspects of the human psyche represented – Doc would recommend against such practices or Operations. Playing with these toys often causes serious psychological injury. It's not a can of worms it's a garbage truck of maggots.

There are many out there who think that these are real entities. Now, maybe there's an invisible world where entities exist – I really cannot say for certain. But it must be understood that what Dr. Zeero is waging war on here is the concept that you should sacrifice devotion to your own Mind Power in favor of communion with an external archetype.

In comparison to the power of The Operator, I feel it's a big waste of time. Doc is trying to show A Better Way, absolutely. Furthermore, when you start wheeling & dealing in all these demons and they're all representations of different states of the inhuman psyche and inhumanity – you're just going to drive yourself insane.

It's the same thing with the Qliphoth, right? Let's let's be honest here – there's no definitive Qliphotic document, there's nothing that came from the Jewish people that really explored it because it was a banned practice. It was just acknowledged that these Husks existed that there was a Shadow Tree, but it isn't it isn't explained much.

The schematic of the Qliphoth that we get in modern days with the Arch Demons of the Husks – that road map is coming from Agrippa's *Three Books of Occult Philosophy*. Even though there isn't a section on the Qliphoth there's a section on the Sephirot and it lists what the Arch Demon of each is. This list has been continually pushed for centuries yet nobody knows where Agrippa got his source.

The Demonic Rulers that are all attributed to the different Sephirot – this is probably just Christianized stuff. This is also the beginning of Lucifuge because The Lord Of Pacts doesn't exist anywhere else in any religious document. Then he just pops up again in *The Red Dragon* (another joke) where his proper name is allegedly "Rofocale." What's the source on this one? Some French guy printing a shock pamphlet to make a buck. Research it.

All these infamous Black Magick Grimoires – they're all a ridiculous joke. Plus all this Medieval spirit conjuring claptrap where you cast a circle of protective Hebrew God names to guard you from the demon that you're summoning in a triangle before you. This arrogance where you assume a demonic entity will appear in subservience to your Holy Purity and that you can materialize & control it as if a lion tamer. *Bogus!*

Another thing – the obsession with Sex Magick. There's power there, obviously, and sexuality isn't something that Doc chastises. Doc here is a sex positive person ethically that just doesn't participate. Celibacy has made my own Mind Power stronger than ever before.

You know, I think Lilith is a really bad idea. Not that Lilith isn't about self-empowerment or revolting against enslavement (theoretically). It's just this narrow obsession with sexual energy & prowess & bouncing & gurgling & gargling. Just aim higher dude.

Being a Supervillain means never having to say you're sorry – it means you can just say whatever seemingly absurd balderdash you want all the time and since you don't give a rat's arse about what anyone thinks, then hallelujah it's a miracle of super ego.

We must get to the root of something near & dear to Doc's blackened heart – the marriage of Satanism + Supervillainy. Despite being a friendly to all Satanists, Doc Zeero is not actually a Satanist. That label once applied perhaps, but it was outgrown long ago.

In fact Zeero Xiron represents the evolution of such philosophy & spirituality. See, Doc presents A New Path – one that blast to bits all the weaknesses of Satanism in every possible way. What would that be? Well Supervillainy there, Silly Pants! When you go full Supervillain, every philosophy crashes to ruin because you become the scribe of reality.

Your ego and your Magickal Vision become totalitarian – it doesn't matter what the world thinks because you are a conqueror of the world. Your ego is the axis on which the globe spins. And hot damn do things get fun fast! Everything is rendered Amusement Park. The rest of the world? Screw 'em – that Ferris Wheel is all yours.

The major flaw of Satanism (whether Symbolic or Theistic) is that it projects all manner of wisdom onto the figure of Satan – something that ultimately is separate from yourself. The major flaw is that you are being humble. Satanism teaches you to be loud & proud, to dominate all situations.

On a long enough timeline, what is left but to rebel against Satanism itself? Quite simply – F**K Satan. As a Magickal Supervillain you are beyond Satan. On the Theistic end, you must recognize if you are ever to evolve that death is a prison and Satan is your prison bitch. Furthermore, the Satan "as a symbol only" aesthetic – it is self-degrading & counterproductive to accept that Satan is somehow more hardcore than you are.

A true Supervillain has no need of Satan, because a true Supervillain is Satan. It's an upgrade! As a Supervillain, you are the light and the darkness. You are The Architect of the reality about you and as a Supervillain you warp it completely to your own megalomaniac specifications.

All Gods crumble before you; there is not a demonic entity worth your time, for they all learn from you. It is Azazel who approaches you for The Flaming Sword. It is you whom Zalmoxis seeks to be a pupil of vampirism. It is you who rewrites The Commandments. Understand as a Supervillain you own reality – The Game is yours. You roll The Nickels, you stack The Cards.

I know it's hard to divorce Satan overnight. It takes time to break up with that lunkhead. But let me tell you – Satan doesn't have shite on the raw power of your own creative mind. That is the point of being the Magickian – you are The Operator, you are the strongest. All these demons & angels & supernatural beings – they are your automatons. Want to go full Supervillain Sorcerer? Simply conclude that all demons are in fact your henchmen because they all work for you. In the Hierarchy of Hell you are Top Dog...

Now to an integral subject – talking about henchmen. So what is a henchman? Well, a faithful follower or political supporter prepared to engage in crime or dishonest practices by way of service. We are expanding this definition into the realm of Magick.

See, Aleister Crowley knew what was up. He was a manufacturer of henchmen and promoted himself as a Supervillain long before the concept existed – *trailblazer!* Another Magick madman warping the world in his own twisted image with his own nefarious ideology and still they follow him today.

But his message is ultimately drivel, unlike Doc here who actually presents you the way of Global Magickal Domination. Believe you me – that Holy Guardian Angel he speaks of is no other then our collective Batman. Avoid gnosis like the plague. Learn what you can from Crowley and then make him walk the plank. No room for canned ham on your ship.

See, Doc doesn't have friends, he has henchmen – willing or unwilling, knowing or unknowing – everyone works for me just as they should work for you too. But how? Well, here's some "Henchmen 101."

Firstly, there needs to be a huge reward for withstanding your program. You best have something to deliver, because Bargain Basement Hustlers rarely last long. Secondly, if you are a male Supervillain, then charisma is the sustaining force.

If you are a female Supervillain, remember that charming, hypnotic seduction is your greatest asset. Men are stupid as bricks – they are easily manipulated by glamour so use their crotch intelligence buffoonery against them. If you aren't a supermodel Supervillain don't you fret – it's your personal power that makes you attractive. Beauty is in the eye of the beholder and being a Supervillain means you replace peoples eyeballs with your own sight. You force the henchmen to see only your Grand Vision.

Now, you ask, what makes a great henchman? Well, loyalty to manifesto, not to greed. A henchman chasing money can never be trusted. They can be utilized but they are auxiliaries. Don't know what I mean? Read Machiavelli.

All henchmen are ultimately disposable canon fodder. You have to mold them, move them like pawns & sacrifice accordingly. The chess pieces you wanna hang onto – your rooks, bishops, knights – these are your Mini-Bosses. As in those on their way up the ladder to the true Supervillainhood. You have to keep them on a tight leash though, lest they overthrow you. Those individuals are another discussion entirely.

For now, we explore rank and file henchmen. Why low level henchmen? Because they carry out your dastardly vision there, Silly Pants. They do things for ya. Every Supervillain needs a cadre of throwaway henchmen. Always remember when you step up and become a Supervillain, everyone in the world works for you – but choose carefully.

Those most enthusiastic to become Supervillain henchmen you will find in the subcultures of Punk Rock, Heavy Metal and Goth Industrial. But a word of warning – Oogles make shitty henchmen. They can't get anything right. Give 'em a mission and next thing you know they are off the clock, spanjing coins for Steel Reserve outside the liquor store. If you must utilize an Oogle, make sure they are a tweeker. A drunken Oogle is useless, a tweeker Oogle has spunk. But they can't be trusted to carry out the most important missions.

Moving on from Oogles we get way more bright types. Problem is, so many Punk kids are crusaders. They adopt the "Scene Police" Superhero ethos. You can't have them figure out your secret Supervillain masterplan, cause they'll try to stop ya.

If you have to go dirty, go sub-Oogle. The Scumfuc kids are the gnarliest grunts who are always down, but you have to keep them fueled on booze & drugs. And they will annoyingly speak in the language Toilet Rock. They are boring is what I mean, and Supervillains need constant intellectual stimulation. Scumfuc's = quick fix for Dirty Deeds.

Now Heavy Metal henchmen – good choice. Probably the best choice. At least they have cars, jobs & apartments. They beer it up and not meth it down. So this leaves the industrial folks. Now these types, many secretly wish to be Sith Lords. So exploit that shit. They wanna work for the Emperor, so show them your inner Palpatine.

Continuing your Super Value Psychological Shopping Experience for all your Sinister Supervillain Needs, the next topic is something integral to Supervillain subculture – split personalities! As they say – two heads are better than one!

It is no coincidence that we get the following piece of mail from Brandon Teasley of San Diego, California. Brandon writes: *"Dear Doc – battling society with my secret Supervillain schemes can be a little challenging to put it lightly. I have yet to be diagnosed with a split personality because my dark reflection informs me to never snitch on it to psychiatric professionals. Thus far I've flown under the radar..."*

"Life was quite Helter Skelter before, but trying to get Jekyll & Hyde to equally cooperate is utterly draining and often futile. What advice can you give a fella who struggles with such opposites? I ask now while I am fully in control. I hope to surprise my quote / unquote brother with a special broadcast from my favorite Supervillain monologue master Dr Zeero Xiron. I'm sure he will appreciate it + good luck with whatever game of chess you are playing there on YouTube! I'm sure your cunning Supervillain logic can win the battle. Cheers & Thanks for the wild ride – your show is lollipops & skittles!"

Well thank you there, uh, Brandon – I'm enthusiastic to help sort out your Duality. Now first off, legitimate split personalities are something of a large undercurrent in Supervillain subculture, so let's just take an objective step back and examine some more famous examples of this issue.

Firstly, you should not be ashamed of multiple selves. You didn't start that way, but you surely ended up that way. If the Mental Health Establishment eyes you are sick and need help – often against your own Wills – things can be treacherous. On the other hand, as a Supervillain it's a strength that drives you so either you run from your own shadow or you embrace it fully.

In Witchcraft and Magick we call it "Shadow Work" – but sometimes you find you have a Second Shadow with a life all its own. Sometimes you have several. It all depends on who comes to the door at any given moment. Hell, sometimes you don't even know who or what will take the wheel so the logical discussion should be safeguards.

Let's talk Harvey Dent and Norman Osborne. Now, Osborne has no safeguard except psychiatric pills of suppression. When he forgets to take them he just launches off on a hovercraft dressed like a goblin – the Green Goblin – throwing pumpkin bombs at people. Of all the ways a split personality could materialize, that is quite an interesting aesthetic choice.

Now Harvey on the other hand – Two Face – he doesn't bother to hide; he's loud and proud about it. Instead of pills he's got his coin – bad side / good side, one flip and it's decided. But his flaw is that without the coin he cannot make up his minds. Knock that circular silver out of his hands then Harvey is just useless & scrambling.

We have to give a round of applause to the doctors at Arkham Asylum – they found out how to help Harvey. The coin is two options only; they took it away and he couldn't figure out if he had to use the toilet or not – he kept soiling his drawers, you know? He just he couldn't make up his Minds. So to extend his options they gave him a 52 pack of playing cards. 52 options, not just 2. Doc suggests you start there. A 52 headed Hydra is better than a conjoined twin.

Green Goblin there – don't expect much change. Sometimes split Supervillains get stuck in their ways. I mean what screams lost cause more than Green Goblin? Psycho – total psycho. Hilarious to watch, terrible to team up with.

A psychopath of this sort is not a professional; they are a wild card. You just gotta let them go their own way like Mama Bird pushing baby bird out the nest to fly that first time. So yes, the Goblins out there take flight – just be careful when attempting to seriously organize them into a formidable force.

Now back to the 52 options... Truth is as a Magickal Supervillain you can do better. You have to fixate on one major tool of your Magickal Arsenal – the 78 card Tarot deck. This opens a whole new universe of split navigation. It's really like getting 78 Two Face coins with one side scratched (Qliphoth) and one side mint (Ēṣ Ḥayyīm). Hence, one Tarot reversed & one upright.

And then you factor in all the deep Occult wisdom each card represents to offer you a fully illuminated range of paths to take. An entire Universe opens up to you – quick results! So I hope this helps Brandon, I highly recommend the Rider-Waite Deck – it has the most comprehensive imagery available on the market. When you are a Supervillain using Tarot, remember both Death and The Tower are the 2 best cards you can draw...

You really gotta work for your Supervillainy – it doesn't just happen. It's like running the marathon. You gotta warm up – get your ham strings ready, do the yoga stretches. You gotta be hyped up & sharp as a tack.

All Supervillains – we got a symbiotic relationship. When united it's this thing known as the "Supervillain Team Up" and there's different versions. We need to talk about what could be seen as the "Supervillain International." Because we all need to gather & connive together – masterplans & ways of distorting reality & sticking it to The Man. 'Cause remember, The Man is gonna come after us like vigilantes. There's also Magickal Superheroes out there who take themselves way too serious and they don't like our antics.

We have to have a dialogue if any of us are to unite forces in Supervillain Sorcery. Can we adopt a platform or organization? When you look at the comic books, you have the Injustice League and, you know, they are always fighting & quibbling & backstabbing each other cause they are Supervillains. That's the thing – can't always trust each other. Lot of lying & cheating & stealing involved.

We should have a global truce. I don't know what that truce would be but there should be an attempt of formulation. You know, Jesus is our punching bag – but Jesus never fights back. It's just people yelling at you with signs and stuff. Or they are just screaming at you on a street corner, and its always fun getting into a shouting match. But it isn't very productive. You cannot win an argument with a madman.

More often then not, Supervillain Internationals never really work out. Generally because you need some Ultra-Baddie to run it and this creates a multi-issue cataclysmic event series. Onslaught is a great example, or Apocalypse.

What makes Supervillain Team Ups such a pain in the arse is that the things that make people Supervillains – all the freakish things that happened to them – well we're talking about the Magickal Vision fueled with what some may deem abnormal psychology. Supervillains, we're just different, you know?

But there is the element of greed, and one could suggest greed of the Magickal Vision. Greed of all encompassing fanaticism. What I'm saying is it's difficult to navigate this extreme greed of Supervillainy. It's a pitfall, assuredly.

As I noted about these Satanist groups and their ideologies – when you become your own God you essentially become dictator of the self. You become dictator of your own mind, body & spirit all combined – it's a form of your territory. And you have to be an Iron Fisted Tyrant of your own belligerent self empire. You become self-imperialist by nature. Supervillains – we'll fight dirty to get what we want, you know?

So these Supervillain conferences are like meetings between feuding, volatile countries attempting to form treaties. Never trust another Supervillain. You can have adventures together, but keep an eye on 'em.

Working with Supervillains is much different then henchmen or Mini-Bosses. When the chips are down you'll see their true colors. So it's always important to be mindful of abandoning your relationships to other Supervillains before they themselves are backed in a corner and sell you out instead.

It would behoove you to keep your wits – if they aren't self serving, they are fanatically self righteous in service of something far more zonky then their superego. It is important to note that if it is greed or zealotry that defines the other Supervillains you're dealing with, then it is always most fortuitous when your zealotry aligns.

Also note the range of Magick Techniques used – you really want a symbiotic relationship with people who can compliment you. A further observance – you will know a Supervillain by their henchmen. It's important to scrutinize this factor. Also, you need to ponder what kind of world domination are they seeking, and why?

Many Supervillains don't even call themselves such but are nonetheless the archetype in political life or oligarchy. Elon Musk is a perfect fit – mad scientist, rich, all types of wild designs on the world, throwing the Nazi Salute and lying about it just to tickle the balls of the Proudly Boys. He's reorganizing your society. So perfect example why you don't always want to align yourself with just any Supervillain. Just cause we're rebellious criminals doesn't mean we don't have any ethics.

Also, consider Supervillain aesthetic razzmatazz. Like how are they dressing, how are all their uniforms going together? What is the motif? It's kind of a runway and you're a bit of a model. You really gotta show it off.

Either you get swallowed by the other bigger fish, or you are the King Leviathan. And when you swim with the sharks, a true Supervillain is always a Leviathan. Which brings us to "Supervillain Proselytization." A henchmen becomes a Mini-Boss and when they reach that point you have to send them off to start their own Supervillain franchises.

If you keep your Mini-Bosses hanging around too long and they get too strong, they overthrow you and they take control of the Syndicate, right? So what you need to do is send them off unto the world to create new cells and beautiful things will happen.

Remember that most Supervillains have fragile egos. Avoid sad boy Supervillains, cause they're whiny. Avoid emo Supervillains. You can usually tell them by the haircut & heavy mascara. They're gonna break down crying, they're gonna feel mighty inadequate. You need a hard-assed Supervillain but not an Edge Lord, cause that shit's annoying. They never stop trying to prove how Punk Rock they are. But hey, can you blame them? What's more Punk Rock then going full on Supervillain?

You don't gotta wear a cape, but I would suggest a mask. Not that it's needed, it's just way more comfortable. That's why Doc wears masks. It's not that I'm hiding my face or I'm trying to scare people, it's just I'm more comfy. That's where I feel like I am centered. Some people have their safety blanket, some people have their Halloween masks. And I just wear 'em around the house. And people look at me funny and they think I've lost my mind. Maybe I have. But I've found my mind many times. It just changes every time I find it.

Also it helps to get a filthy rich industrialist guy up to no good nefarious plots in your corner. Rich guy, has political motivations, has fantastic connections. Guys like that are always looking to hire Supervillains. They pick you out to use you because they think they can control you but you just turn around and use them instead. Easy peazy.

Like with Bane in *Dark Knight Rises* when that dude is like, *"Why are my men running around the city, blah blah blah?"* and Bane is like, *"Do you really feel in charge?"* and he just snaps that guy's neck? So use them for what they're worth. Use their garbage trucks, use their men – but remember you're the one in charge.

Also, keep in mind there's the whole thing of tricking the public into sympathy with you, in case you want to run for political office. Fool the public, save a baby – that's it, works every time. You just need to somehow do that in front of a speculative public; get it in the newspapers and they will adore you. Also quote / unquote "publicly forgive your parents." That trash works great on the Rubes. And then, run for Mayor.

Dr Zeero has a vision. I hope this Vision also infects you all because it has a little bit to do with Green Magick. Because of all the Paradigm hopping and high fallutin' High Magick, it's important to peel it back just to Nature.

Nothing makes you more filled with the surge of Green than being in the forest. And as I walk the concrete of my nightmare city and think about it's black top & steel – you know, I just look around and I see what mankind has done. Those controlling us have cut down every single possible tree that grows fruit.

It started in the South – they freed the Slaves who immediately went to wild orchards. So they galloped in and cut them all down. Then came our modern days – the hobo camps & desperation of the Great Depression. Hacked down when people needed it the most.

Trees are the essence of stopping hunger. It's a no brainer. There's no reason anybody should be hungry whatsoever because it grows on trees. And our cities – everywhere you go should be strawberry bushes & blackberries & orange trees & apple trees & whatever else. Everywhere you go should be a garden.

This is the simpleton vision of Dr Zeero – there shouldn't be concrete everywhere. We should be living in a garden paradise. We should be collecting nuts and berries – that should be our entire economy! *Endless harvest & free rationing!* We could have made it an entire agriculture based society and the whole point was to feed our people with a fair share but, uh, I guess it's called Communism.

The sheer absurdity of the world is what I'm talking about. The second they made ordinances where you couldn't light your own fires within City Limits they took away your ability to make fire. Do you realize how the Deep the repercussions are? They neutered us as a hunter / gatherer species, shackled us to their concrete hellscapes.

It's to the point where in the middle of winter you have freezing homeless under bridges and the cops are forcing them to put out the fires keeping them alive because the city ordinance takes precedence over frostbite, over misery, over survival.

When I was a little kid it was this this time period called the 1980s. The 80's & 90's – we always assumed the sci-fi dystopian future would be inserting microchips in our skin so that in order to shop or use money, rent a home, do anything at all – we would have to present this chip for authorization. Jump to now – what was it really? Our Smart Phones.

It was not just a microchip they herded us with but a fully functioning brain in your hand. So they could study you & know everything about you & know your every move & algorithm you. They handed us the Internet as well, combining both into the perfect mechanism for control.

Give a dope enough rope and they'll hang themselves every time. Just give us the shiny new toy – we're going to play with it for a very, very long time until it's completely embedded in our daily lives. Now they use Facebook against you in court.

All the new laws that this borderline fascist state has put into practice – the blank check to rampant authoritarianism that President Chump has handed law enforcement & military & I.C.E. – it is jarring & totalitarian.

Everything we Leftists ever warned you folks about happening if you didn't pay attention, didn't show up and vote and let these sort of people get into power – it's all happened. It's a textbook definition by-the-book authoritarian takeover.

We are split down the middle – half of America rejects this Vision. That's the difference between this attempt of a wannabe dictatorship – you have a zeitgeist of backlash in opposition. This nationalist, militaristic buffoon probably wants a Hermit Kingdom like a big ol' Chump Hotel Resort Complex. Like a sick Disneyland suppressed by the whims of a lunatic old man playing with war toys and gambling with that which he absolutely should not be gambling with alongside all kinds of psychotic policies.

Even here and there where he will do things that make sense "on paper" that could be good for the country in a different context – understand if 90% of the decisions are very poor decisions, bad management decisions, bad policy decisions, bad strategy creating bad influences making the economy harder & creating unnecessary trade war & launching more aggressive strikes on different countries – how can you preach the non-involvement of American Interventionalism?

Frank Zappa was right – the number one threat to America was ignoring the basis for a fascist theocracy incrementally rising in America as evidenced by the Moral Majority and the whole Evangelical base. George Carlin was right too because he talked about when fascism returned it would be in sneakers. Well how about Red Hats?

If you're 100% on the side of President Chump I don't know what to say to you. Even lunatics who are gonna flush their country down the toilet will still pull a few winners out their ass. Not everyone can have totally asinine ideas all the time – you can just be boiled over with mostly asinine ideas and still have a few good ones. I guess if you're thrilled to live in a military police state where Homeland Security runs everything, this is your Golden Era.

You can't Urban Camp anymore – it's illegal to sleep outside on public or federal property. It's illegal to be homeless! They're talking about making camps, basically just concentration camps from where you are eventually processed into Government Project buildings. You get 2 years to work a job & reintegrate to society & secure your own rental situation. If you fail then what? It's illegal to be homeless again and you are marked? You're not allowed to go back to the FEMA tent cities? Do you get deported to Guantanamo?

You should vote me as President. That's it – President Zeero. I'd do a better job, guaranteed. I can say that with full authority...

Anyway... If I drag this on too much longer I'm going to lose your interest and I'm just going to get more ranty than I was maybe previously, so once again, thanks for stopping by the Dr. Zeero Xiron Free Magick Secrets Show where we investigate all forms of Magick.

You should hit the "videos tab" & scroll down – there's like 300+ videos to learn from cause this is a Magick School that's FREE with all kinds of FREE Magick Secrets all the time, for all the good lil' Boys & Girls & Non-Binary young 'uns out there.

I promise that if you listen to everything from start to finish you will have a full wizardly education. You're going to be like a Medieval Sorcerer guy – you're gonna be on another level, right? That's the way it's going to work. Just trust me.

So anyway, post these videos on Facebook or Reddit or Twitter or whatever social media platform you use – blah blah blah / yakkity smakkity. As always, Hail Arkham & here's your Hot Rocking Outro. Later kids...

(Hot Rocking Outro = Karl Casey @ White Bat Audio)

– Appendix –
"Propaganda In Motion"
(by Zeero Xiron)

PROPAGANDA

Invoking War & Spreading Lies, the technique called "Propaganda" has long been a centerpiece of systematic manipulation. It comes in many forms – sometimes obvious & blatant, and other times smooth, subtle & coy.

Propaganda means "To Propagate" – any image with a "secret message" intended to influence behavior, emotion or ideas.

"Propaganda" is not the Evil War Poster in itself, nor the Corrupt Government trying to manipulate its citizens into military service.

In short, Propaganda is the "Magickal Will" of an Image.

It is a "Fixed Magickal Will" intentionally created and layered into an image as to provoke a definite emotional influence, physical response, or to reinforce (or "seed") a specific idea.

Yet is also takes form by way of language itself; your words are like Propaganda devices meant to create a Billboard in the recipients mind that forever broadcasts your message requiring action. It also takes form in Audio – every note and tonality is a Propaganda of impression that works on the psyche.

The point is to Seed an Idea; to grow your Garden, per se.

In this general understanding there really is no difference between, say, a "Magickal Talisman/Amulet" that invokes an essence in it's wearer, or evokes a specific reaction by another person viewing it.

As with Magick & Witchcraft, Propaganda can be White, Black or Grey. Thus, Propaganda in itself isn't a "bad thing" or "evil manipulation" – it simply means intentional influence.

Yet the knee-jerk response from most uninformed people when simply hearing the word "Propaganda" is to recoil in disgust or distrust, as if hearing the words of a Corrupt Snake tempting one to devour the Poisoned Fruits of a Diseased Tree.

This is a fatal error, for "Advertising" & "Propaganda" are essentially the same – identical, actually. The reason we distinguish the two is because "Advertising" is simply the "soft word" adopted by the economic world.

People inherently get upset when you "Fool Them," or when they realize you are trying to "Fool Them" on purpose – no matter what it is about. Most of the time, the ones most upset are those most easily fooled.

For these people, there is selective process of ignoring information that they've self-willed & self-trained purposely as to "look the other way." In short, they find the sheer bombardment of advertisements systematically manipulating them horrifically creepy, and want no further consideration.

This is a dismal response that finds no balance with the brighter equation.

For instance, imagine you are walking down the street and encounter a billboard advertisement that shows an image of smiling people all Democratically voting in a free and fair election. The not-so-hidden message propagated is: "please vote in a free election."

Is there any reason to fear this message because it has been "propagandized" to you? Are you not happy to see this billboard seeding this specific idea, as opposed to some Dictator's billboard seeding tyranny?

Do you yourself not use your words as if a sonic billboard? If you speak the sentence "go vote in a free and fair election" to your friend and say it with vibrant, emotional charge and they act on it, does your sentence in their memory not constitute an "inner plane" billboard? A sentence etched in the memory like a fixed object with a fixed Magickal Will, forever in the subconscious computer, eternally repeating the same message?

Are you not putting unconscious advertisements in people's minds anytime you want to "fire them up" to do something you believe in, such as community work? Does it not feel like you've accomplished the right thing by inciting 12 people to show up and feed/clothe the homeless on a freezing winter day, when they otherwise would've sat at home watching TV?

But you, as Master Propagandist, propagated this action? By appealing to their emotions as to influence their direct behavior and mold it so they will hand out clean socks, soup cups and blankets?

Similarly, one could find a billboard showing The Amazon Forest being destroyed by developers and attempting to influence the viewer into some sort of action towards protecting the environment.

The above examples clearly show why Propaganda is not "The Villain" – it is the agenda and intention of "The Operator" that must be questioned.

As with Magick & Witchcraft, Propaganda can be White, Black or Grey.

In realization of this, the clever mind will quickly discern that every time they step into public they are besieged with Magickal Manipulation from all manners of advertisers & systems. Once you train your mind to locate the Propagandic Layers, you begin to see things very clearly.

A Pop Culture reference to this phenomenon is best described by "They Live." Propaganda is a form of literacy – and when you are able to "Read Propaganda" you begin to see things as Roddy Piper did, with those wonderful sunglasses on.

Other modes of Propaganda are quite subtle. One can easily imagine Military Posters attempting to recruit soldiers – but not so often is it recognized that Commercial Advertisements are also Propaganda.

Propaganda occurs anytime an artist paints a picture that intentionally conveys a secret message – art with a message that the viewer decodes subliminally.

"Propagating The Message" in art is often purely emotional. If a painting is meant to evoke a specific emotional response, that is it's "Propagandic Function."

If the artist "Captured The Feeling Perfectly" it's because the Propaganda worked effectively, because the Propagation was "The Feeling."

Anytime a Punk Rock band writes a song against "Manipulative War Propaganda," they are using Propaganda. The recorded song, like a static image, has a fixed "Magickal Will" to it – it's "set in stone" forever, intentionally, because The Operators (The Band) created it to be that way.

In Punk Rock, the lyrical messages are generally direct. But anytime lyrics are vague enough that the listener has to demystify it and come to an analytical conclusion as to what the poetic language means (*and the writer of the lyrics/song knew the listener was going to puzzle over the material before arriving at a preconceived conclusion of ideas*), it is Text Book Propaganda

Despite this author having spent decades involved in Punk Rock, it has often been the author's experience that Punk Rockers get really freaked out when you even mention the word "Propaganda" because they've been conditioned (rightfully) to have a knee-jerk reaction to the word.

The reason why is because Punk Rock bands have from the start of their subculture been propagating through Propaganda that a certain *form* of Propaganda is bad. And they are absolutely correct to do so – yet it obscures the larger dynamic.

**Understand that this thesis itself is from an Author who is attacking "manipulative Propaganda" with the same zeal & ferocity of a Punk Rock protest song, and also an author who's political opinions are left wing. Furthermore, consider this not just an average "Punk Rock tune," but more a crusty C-Tuned Grindcore blast attack with ripping Thrash Metal guitars.

Therefore, understand The Author's general attitude when commenting that anytime a Punk Rocker wears Punk Rock clothing as to visually declare they are rebelling against conformity (*whatever that personally means to them), they are wearing Propaganda to propagate this message.* For the Punk Rock scene, Propaganda is their ultimate power and resource.

That may not sit well with people, but let's be honest. There is no scene more expert in utilizing Propaganda to make itself grow then Punk Rock. The zines, t-shirts, bumper stickers, symbols, iconography; the wild hair colors & loud clothing – these are all vehicles of Propaganda to propagate a message about revolting against static conformity.

No scene is more aggressive about warning & educating people on the manipulative Propaganda of The State then the Punk Rockers.

But the Punk Rock scene made a unfortunate error by convincing themselves that all forms of Propaganda are to be attacked & criticized outright, and to not even investigate or educate themselves on the concept.

Yet still they use Propaganda as their ultimate tactic, and it stands at the center of their entire art form and community.

Heavy Metal is another subculture that echoes many underpinning elements of Punk Rock, and the two are like rival siblings which are interconnected.

However, where Punk Rock concentrates it's message more on protesting the injustices of the physical world and tangible subjects – the Heavy Metal scene is more about Empowerment of The Self Will as the ultimate protest.

The Metalheads are largely aware of "Magickal" ideas, because the Occult was always a "cool" topic in their subculture, going all the way back to Black Sabbath & Led Zepplin. Even the most uneducated metalhead still thinks like a Ceremonial or Alchemical Magickian – the question is how expansive is their knowledge. The Goth/Industrial world is similarly saturated in Occult exploration.

Therefore, Propaganda becomes a tool which can ultimately bridge these subcultures and create mutual pro-activity for positive change & dynamism.

Another example of unnoticed Propaganda are Movies. When we watch a film, we are being bombarded with images that have specific influence. One can hit pause and study a frame to derive information.

This is the craft of the Filmmaker. "Film Literacy" – as in you can clearly "read" what is being communicated through the picture (*as well as facial expressions, dialogue, accompanying music, character drives, etc*).

Films are highly controlled, massive assortments of Propaganda strung together to leave it's audience with a final summarized idea, perception or feeling – the "Propagandic Bottom Line," per se.

The Director/Writer/Producer/Editor all intertwine as one Master Propagandist. The finished product is the work of a Propaganda Collective which essentially coagulate into a larger blanket Propagandist. They all form the "Wizard Of Oz" behind their work.

Some films can be watched on mute and easily understood via "Film Literacy" (aka Propaganda Literacy). This is when a person can clearly "read between the lines" or actively seeks to discern the information while looking at what is blatantly presented to point to the secret message.

Some films have a quiet meaning that is never explicitly stated. One example is "Taxi Driver." On surface it seems a film about a troubled vigilante. Yet at core, we are being told information that says: "You are watching a complex mental illness you do not fully understand going off in a logically illogical way, and if you watch what Travis says/does, we are given clues to it's larger orientation."

So as one can see, the importance is understanding that Propaganda is about the conveyance of ideas, and is omnipresent – and is often called something else as not to confuse it or stigmatize it with blatant Propaganda of the state or what we generally recognize Propaganda as.

Defined by American Heritage as "*The systematic proposition of a given Doctrine or of allegations reflecting its views and interests*," Propaganda is the advertising of ideas, of philosophy, and of ideology.

However you evaluate it, the purpose is that of a deliberate, refined attempt to shape perceptions, mold behavior, or alter/maintain a balance of power that is advantageous to the Propagandist or system behind it.

We also find it's predominance in the rituals of organized religion, with their symbols of sanctity & divinity, which are also a form of Propaganda. The term itself comes from Latin: "Congregation De Propaganda Fide" (*congregation for propagating Roman Catholicism*).

It is unalterable that such a concept is ultimately linked with an objective to transmit ideology to an audience with related convictions or to persuade those yet concretely affirmed in their views.

Yet the stigma that always takes precedence – *does Propaganda mean lies*?

The theories, ideas & opinions presented in this work are ultimately aimed at social, cultural & artistic progress. The over-arching goal is to communicate the possibility of an apolitical framework which would induce a stronger & more unified underground through both knowledge and application of Propaganda in all its conceivable forms.

This thesis rests entirely upon certain assumptions which will in effect be recognized as the principle guidelines of all henceforth presented ideas.

1. The belief that all forms of ideology, religion, advertising, and political systems are ultimately Propaganda vying for the support of the individual.

2. An understanding that the Modern Pagan Renascence is undeniably linked in its growth to Propaganda. Not simply by virtue "As Above, So Below," but also the very nature of Global Community. Whenever we intentionally advertise "Community" by means of flyers, brochures, posters, MEMEs – when we are fully aware that we are attempting to market the idea of "Community" to elicit an enthusiastic response from whomever may be looking at our advertisement – this is Propaganda. "Advertising" is marketing a business service while "Propaganda

is the "hidden message," the "gut feeling," the imparted impression. Propaganda is therefore the Magickal principle of advertising. It is the will of the Propagandist, like the will of the Magician, to create a thought form. And just as a Ceremonial Magician send thought forms into the world, so the Propagandist sends their thought forms by means of imagery cloaked in advertising.

3. As the Global Pagan Community continues to expand with ever-increasing synchronicity. Occult Practitioners of all traditions & philosophies are now viewing themselves as a larger, more dynamic, interconnected whole. In concert with the Digital Age, the advance of internet connectivity has allowed the full range of Magickal traditions from antiquity until present to be researched & absorbed at a rate of acceleration unseen throughout the history of Magick. It is therefore integral to empower, sustain & evolve the growth of our global community by all rational, positive means – and there is no more a potent Magickal tool then by means of Propaganda.

4. The belief that at some level all music is "Audio Propaganda" – either in terms of propagating a direct message, or simply propagating an essence of feeling. If a composer seeks to transmit a specific emotion or mood to a listener as to invoke total sympathy and harmony with his composition, then this would note a classic example. For further exemplification, one not need seek further then the Bardic Schools of Druidry to firmly grip the importance of the uniting principles of Music, Magick & Propaganda as one.

5. The belief that the strongest resistance to Manipulative Propaganda is by studying Propaganda itself, and that through a comprehensive knowledge of its omnipresence one can clearly observe its ability to mold & modify both behavior & physical action.

6. Propaganda is the most vital, unexplored Magickal Technique we have at our disposal to motivate idealism & sustain inertia. It has many long ranging implications to the Pagan Community and our evolving efforts.

7. Once energized, we will be able to confer on new methods of alliance, multi-lateral approaches of activism & social change. Accelerated progress is only ascertainable in the zealous passion of a mass working together with healthy, positive philosophies.

This is not to say such sentiment doesn't exist already or that there is little cooperation. The international underground continues to swell – at every local level worldwide progress is being made with each passing day. It all boils down to the cultivation of raw passion to achieve our shared goals.

Despite the amount of naysayers, the greatest successes in history tend to be those which found the least understanding initially because they stood in starkest contrast with the general public opinion.

Propaganda is a taboo subject, buried from public discourse for a number of reasons. Chiefly, it's suppression is due to it being a communication so powerful that it can, when honed to perfection, sway every mind & soul on earth. If there is a way to unite all minds as one shared psychic mass focusing on one concept, image, or evoked feeling at the same time, it is through the technique of Propaganda, fusing itself to the perfect item.

There cannot be any argument against our inability to bring about total change within our lifetimes, but this does not relieve us in any way the obligation of resistance.

In the question of idealism, past failures mustn't detour us – political parties & social clubs are inclined to compromises, Occultists never.

Therefore a reactionary philosophy is imminent. Such a basis of thought cannot be willing to collaborate with the hostile world of ideas it struggles against – *it must in essence manufacture its replacement.*

Propaganda accelerates change like no other device.

OPPOSING
PROPAGANDA
(*ANALYSIS & ISOLATION*)

To understand opposing Propaganda and its meaning in our daily lives, we must examine its implications.

There is a definitive process of Propaganda rooting in 5 main concepts: *the institution itself, the Propaganda agents thereof, media methods of attainment, cause and effect of social network, and finally, public opinion.*

Propaganda manifests itself as an appeal to the emotions through beliefs, values, attitudes, behavior, and group "norms." These concepts are considered "*anchors*," or the "*pressure points*" of the human psyche.

Resonance is the final variable of the equation, the sum achievement of all Propaganda systems and the sustaining base of all inertia. Resonance is culminated through the inflammation of all conceivable anchors.

Unlike persuasion, resonance is a skillful technique that inspires the recipient to foster budding ideas in response to a domino effect of either obvious or carefully laid subliminal messages.

Effective Propaganda aims for a target audience and all of the anchors which dictate their perceptions, giving expression to the recipients own concerns, tensions, aspirations, etc.

Thus, Propaganda denies all distance between the source and the audience by mirroring the propagandees own feelings.

Likewise – in the case of public oratory – personal identification must take place between the Propagandist and the propagandee (*recipient*).

They share common sensations, concepts, images, and ideas that make them appear as one. The Propagandist is then an archetypal figurehead that represents the inner voice of the propagandee.

conversely, the propagandic message is more often homogeneous for the mass audience rather than to one person in an interpersonal setting

In regards to this, one must be aware that all institutional Propaganda is manufactured with concealed purpose & identity to establish control of information, manage public opinion, or manipulate behavior in general.

all governments, societies, religions, philosophies and advertisements are unalterably Propaganda mechanisms

The way to resist Propaganda is to identify the ideology & purpose of the campaign, the context in which it appears, the identity & motive of the Propagandist, and the structure of the organization

In terms of "Counter Spelling" Manipulative Propaganda, the famous phrase "Fight Fire With Fire" is adequate. The only way to truly defeat the omnipresent sway of Manipulative Propaganda is for someone to assume the role of Propagandist and create a more powerful Rival Propaganda that manufactures the psychological conditions to impair its influence.

The greatest victory the Manipulative Propaganda brokers ever scored was to disseminate the crippling belief that to wield Propaganda oneself would therefore be "stooping to their level" – something dubious, vile & taboo.

Propagandists propagandized that Propaganda was morally wrong & had little uses outside obvious war use – by using Propaganda they successfully propagated that no ordinary citizen should understand the technique.

Propaganda itself – as a concept – provides the means to disrupt & counter Manipulative Propaganda through all communicative applications.

Magick is the art & science of using willpower to mold reality – Propaganda is its equivalent in the world of imagery & varied media.

After all, what are the 22 Tarot Trumps? What are Runes & Sigils?

Propaganda *is* Magick and must be recognized as such.

AUDIO PROPAGANDA

A LOGICAL SYNTHESIS

Long ago, during the 1950's, the American youth was first introduced to rock and roll. As this movement swept the country the possibility of a brave new world was secured through a medium representing a voice all their own.

It was the ground zero bedrock of all resistance culture to come.

The growth of the resistance culture was rapid – primal freedom was electrified by the awakening of an ancient and largely untapped phenomenon:

Audio Propaganda

More than 60 years after "Rock Around The Clock" planted the seeds of Counterculture in the collective mind of the youth, rock and roll – at least in its mass media definition – has become a harmless cacophony of vibrations and expressions. It is now a spectator sport, or one that aims to be, if you follow the guidelines of opposing Propaganda.

However, disruption has not wavered. New subcultures and attitudes rise from obscurity with each passing day. The real challenge is acceleration.

We mustn't deny the power & veracity that is concentrated in this art-form or it's off-shoots. We must magnify the concept of audio Propaganda's (*and associated counterculture artistic/philosophical movements*) ability to incite progressive response as the central inertia of all intertwined movements.

:PROPAGANDA:
A HISTORICAL CONTEXT)

The greatest and most enduring success in the history of Propaganda – and consequently the first subculture movement to develop it's full potential against the institution of its era – is unquestionably Christianity.

The rise of Christianity demonstrates how by skill and understanding of the audience, a specific appeal was engineered that shaped the course of world history.

Christian Propagandists aimed at the least successful areas of the rapidly collapsing Roman empire. The prime target was the disenfranchised & demoralized, the slaves & sheepherders, the criminal & impoverished.

All of this was manufactured to incite fanatical agitation against the system in order to manufacture its replacement with a radically new version of reality, philosophy, morality, purpose, vision & communal structure.

Its status was initially one of hundreds of competing philosophies created in the vacuum after the fall of Rome, and with Christian Propagandists lacking control over the primitive multimedia at the ruling classes disposal, new ideas had to be fostered in the grassroots advertising of ideas.

What differentiated Christian Propagandists from traditional Hebrew Propagandists was the ability and willingness to transfer conventional messages into a newly abbreviated "short attention span" form.

The use of parables, dramatic gestures on the floor of the Temple, the graphic use of metaphor – the seeds on stony ground, the eye of the camel, the shepherd and his flock – and the highly personal experience of using audience members as human metaphors and making them the stars of the attraction fueled the reaction.

It was nearly 4 centuries later that the cross became the symbol of Christianity. Beforehand, two curved intersecting lines symbolizing a fish was widely used. Not only was this symbol easy to draw, it also had mystical overtones in that it derived from an acronym in Greek – "*Jesus Christ, Son of God, savior*" – savior pronounced *ichthus* (fish). The theme of the fish was also the theme for recruitment, as the metaphor was that of "*fisher of men's souls.*"

The fish symbol was used as a secret sign during persecution. As a result it was found scrawled on walls, trees, any place where Christians wished to leave their mark to communicate their increasing numbers of strength to others.

The most significant of all developments that the Christian Propagandists were responsible for was the very concept of "Cellular Proselytization."

Later adopted by Lenin in the Russian Revolution, this is the process of creating groups in every major area of civilization to logistically support the movement at large. In effect, each cell would have its own leaders, and the loyalty/faith of the cell members were solidified by rituals of communion.

The converts then become Propaganda agents in themselves, propelled by zealot conviction. This was exemplified by the choice of 12 disciples as the dedicated core who would carry the message to other groups, who in turn would spread the word through personal contact in a system resembling today's pyramidal marketing schemes.

In the end, Constantine I (*the "final" Roman Emperor*) adopted Christianity for political motives in 313 AD Realizing that the institution could no longer exist in opposition to this omnipresent movement, Christianity became the "official religion" of all Emperors. Not long after it was also adopted by the Germanic tribes who in turn inherited the remnants of the Empire throughout Europe.

Aided by the remarkable infrastructure and lingering communication system of the tattered Empire, Christianity was then utilized as a ubiquitous Propaganda of control. It was subverted to benefit the ruling class and "updated" whenever necessary, effectively undermining the original intentions of the movement.

And still it exists today, channeling our behavior invisibly through a highly developed Propaganda reaching us from remote prehistory.

PROPAGANDA

(*A TECHNICAL PERSPECTIVE*)

From hereon we discuss the technical aspects central to the effective use of Propaganda. Modern Propaganda uses all media available –- press, radio, television, film posters, meetings, door-to-door canvassing, handbills, billboards, speeches, flags, fashion styles, street names, monuments, coins, stamps, books, plays, comic strips, poetry, music, sporting events, cultural events, company reports, libraries, awards and prizes.

Although there are variations and amalgams of the following themes, these seven major devices have become cardinal models of Propaganda. Those devices are *"Glittering Generality,"* *"Transfer," "Testimonial," "Plain Folks," "Card Stacking,"* *"Name Calling,"* and *"Band Wagon."*

Glittering Generality: Associating a concept with a "virtue word" to create both acceptance and approval of the concept.

Transfer The process of transferring the established respect and authority of something into a new concept to provide it a sense of credibility.

Testimonial Consists in having a respected or hated individual publicly announce their favor towards or dislike of a concept.

Plain Folks Convincing the audience that the ideas of the Propaganda are favorable because they are "of the people," the "plain folks."

Card Stacking Involves the selection and use of facts or falsehoods, illustrations or distractions, and logical or illogical statements in order to give the best or worst possible case for an idea, program, person, or product.

Name Calling Giving a concept a bad label and therefore rejecting and condemning it without examining the evidence.

Band Wagon Has as its core theme "*everyone's doing it*."

Ethically, there are three direct classifications of Propaganda in regards to this system – *Gray Propaganda*, *Black Propaganda*, and *White Propaganda*.

White Propaganda is when the source is identified correctly and the information in the message tends to be accurate. White Propaganda is ultimately meant to form a credible union with its audience.

Gray Propaganda is when the source may or may not be identified correctly and the accuracy of the information is uncertain. It is the beginning of slanting information or concepts whose ultimate truth is in the eye of the beholder, walking the line between fact and fiction.

Black Propaganda is when a false source intentionally fabricates deceptions. "Disinformation" or "Yellow Journalism" also falls into this realm, which is the widespread practice of planting news stories designed to weaken adversaries or political rivals.

Opposing nations often rely on Black Propaganda to weaken their adversaries through initiatives of clandestine "PSYOPS" programs, an acronym for "Psychological Operations." As is evident in KGB Cold War activities, the Soviets had secretly planted journalists in major newspapers in every conceivable state outside the Iron Curtain. The USSR even used black Propaganda against themselves to maintain a desired effect.

"Radio Free Hungary" attracted world attention and sympathy in 1956 when the Russians sent tanks into Budapest to silence the anti-communist revolution. RFH's pleas to the USA aroused sympathy from the entire world.

The violent atrocities the Russians were perpetuating against Hungarians were described in graphic detail, and every transmission contained revolutionary messages to rise against the invading force and overthrow the communist regime since the USA had "promised" to militarily support the uprising. In effect the underground nation-wide broadcast had become the "*voice of the people.*"

In reality the station was a fraudulent KGB operation put in effect to embarrass the USA since they had no intention of getting involved. Thus, Russia demonstrated to the world that the United States could not be relied upon to logistically support a country in revolt.

Radio Free Hungary was so effective that the CIA had no idea it was a Propaganda device until long after it ceased broadcasting.

the 4 basic tenements of successful Propaganda come in its finality – that the Propaganda in question is clearly perceived, comprehended, remembered, and ultimately acted upon

The success of its ideas manifest in becoming a widely acknowledged pathology reputed for its effective and practical integration with reality. The final product must invariably hold direct influence as a streamlining of consciousness whereas its influence directly affects the environment of the individual and those interconnected within the sphere of his existence.

Since each Occultist group within the Global Pagan Counterculture inherently exists as a means to find a conclusion (*or viable alternative*) to a central problem, each incarnation of Propaganda must then be tailored for select demographics.

Since every group has its own identity and generally focuses on resisting differing concepts, this must be left to its members to decide the best course of dissemination. It remains relevant so long as it is symbolically spoken in that groups particular language.

the difference between a member and a supporter is that support requires only a passive recognition of an idea, while membership demands an active role

Propaganda aptly works from the standpoint of an idea and makes the supporter ripe for the success of this idea, while the counterculture as a larger entity achieves growth by the persistence of those enacting the idea. The success of an idea roots in the comprehensiveness of the Propaganda to both support struggle and encourage resistance.

the first task of Propaganda is always to win supporters for proactivity – the second is to incite the continuation of Propaganda from those supporters

False concepts & poor knowledge can be eradicated by instruction, the stubborn resistance of emotions never. As an art form Propaganda focuses on the emotions of its audience, as a tool it provides the essential facts needed for motivation.

There are 3 cardinal rules in direct relation to this:

1) Never assume anyone will come to you naturally

2) Never underestimate the apathy of the average individual

3) Never assume that you can force anyone to change completely

Agitation of resistance, in its fiery extremes, will always have the strongest grip on decimating the foundations of the first three rules. As a revolutionary principle, agitation is not employed to tell someone how to live – agitation exists to *incite* them to live.

All great revolutions in history were set in motion by the agitation of the common man. Similarly, all great agitations were the product of clear, strong, artistically superior Propaganda.

whether or not you agree with any of these sources is unimportant – it is the importance of evaluating influence, how sources such as these have provided the fuel of others fires which have inevitably led to chain reactions

The educated Propagandist observes and understands his art from the liberal heights of the ACLU to the anti-humane methodology of the Nazi Party. Drastically polar opposites of course, but both entities agitating resistance through many of the same techniques.

The difference between the noted comparisons are *aggressive blind agitation* and *impassioned voluntary agitation*. In other words, one can be violently thrust into a mob mentality through Propaganda just as easily as a sane recognition of facts and sense of personal responsibility/morality.

"White Propaganda" concentrates solely on impassioned voluntary agitation

In the question of agitating resistance, never overlook the efficiency of simplicity. The best methods are often the most straightforward and stripped down. Over-intellectualism (*which I am clearly guilty of here*) loses the audience rather quickly.

The average individual possesses an enormous forgetfulness, therefore always retain the essential and avoid the non-essential – keep it sharp and pointed while understanding the logic and language of the target audience. This is the finest way to "*preach outside*" the choir.

The written word serves to retain, reinforce and deepen the points of view, the accompanying artwork most effective when aimed at emotions. Melded together they must present a combination of instant inertia. The Propaganda must get beneath the skin until a definitive catharsis is manufactured.

there must always be a method of practical resolution suggestively attached to this – the more the concept appears solvable, the more the inertia will be culminated

In the motivation of dismantling illusions, there must be no half-statements and no doubts. The sustained application of slogans, symbols, and phrases are utilized to drive ideas and images into the very subconscious of the individual.

The most effective Propaganda presents an obstacle and gives a solution which seems practical to attain. Harsh realism is of strongest motivation – the coldest consideration of reality and the warmest embrace of life. A rigorous examination of opposing Propaganda as a spiritual/physical weapon, the abuses of the system, thorough examinations of society/government, the possibility that God does not exist, the view of the world from a purely alienated/scientific/psychological view.

the overall goal is unequivocally that of clearing all possible obstructions from an amplified, international unity

Although this broad statement seems rather ludicrous in its implications, we must acknowledge that a definitive strategy is not necessary – the strength lies in each group's own determination of struggle and sense of purpose.

In effect, each group becomes another gear within the larger machine. In this there is no conscious center of a larger organization – each group is symbolically an organization working independently of one another in shared philosophy.

PROPAGANDA IN MOTION

From here the organic process becomes self-sustaining. The effective organizer stresses the significance of exhibition, creating his events around a fantastical atmosphere – an alternate world separate of conditioned reality.

When this feeling is successfully conveyed the general audience will carry with them an air of pure disillusionment with all that does not concern this new impassioned reality.

the end result of the organizer's effectiveness will not come from profitable enterprise but rather the creation of more organizers from the inertia culminated

PROPAGANDA IN MOTION: REQUIEM

ARTICLE II: METHODS OF AUDIO Propaganda
(USE OF Propaganda MECHANISMS IN LYRICAL ORATORY)

AD HOMINEM [ARGUMENT TO THE MAN]: Attacking the person instead of attacking his argument. A common form is an attack on sincerity or to attack a whole class of people (power elite vs. the poor). Similarly, waving away a whole category of evidence. Another variation is attack by innuendo.

NEEDLING: Attempting to make the other person angry without trying to address the argument. Sometimes this is a delaying tactic. Needling is also Ad Hominem if you insult your opponent. You may instead insult something the other person believes in, interrupt, clown to show disrespect, or be noisy. If it is your radio show you can cut off the other person's microphone. If the host is on your side that is almost as good as running the show yourself. It's even better if the debate is videotaped, and you are the person who will edit the video.

STRAW MAN [FALLACY OF EXTENSION]: Attacking an exaggerated or caricatured version of your opponent's position. It is also common to exaggerate the opponent's position so that a comparison can be made between the opponent and Hitler, or fascism in general.

INFLATION OF CONFLICT: Arguing that scholars are in debate of a specific point because their entire field of knowledge is "in crisis."

ARGUMENT FROM ADVERSE CONSEQUENCES [FEAR TACTICS]: Saying an opponent must be wrong, because if he is correct then horrible things would therefore ensue. "God must exist, because a godless society would be lawless and dangerous."

SPECIAL PLEADING [STACKING THE DECK]: Using the arguments that support your position, but ignoring/disallowing arguments against it.

EXCLUDED MIDDLE [FALSE DICHOTOMY; BIFURCATION]: Assuming there are only two alternatives when in fact there are many more.

SHORT TERM VS. LONG TERM: Presenting the idea that no two large-scale challenges can coincide.

BURDEN OF PROOF: The claim that whatever has not yet been proved false must be true.

ARGUMENT BY QUESTION: Asking your opponent a question which does not have a quick answer. The opponent has no choice but to appear weak/ill-informed or "heady" & long-winded. Variants are the "rhetorical question" and the "loaded question."

ARGUMENT BY RHETORICAL QUESTION: Asking a question in a way that leads to a particular answer.

FALLACY OF THE GENERAL RULE: Assuming that something true in general is true in every possible case.

REDUCTIVE FALLACY [OVERSIMPLIFICATION]: Over-simplifying. As Einstein said, everything should be made as simple as possible, but no simpler. Political slogans such as "Taxation is theft" fall in this category.

GENETIC FALLACY [FALLACY OF ORIGINS/VIRTUE]: If an argument/ arguer has a specific origin, then that argument must be right (or wrong). The idea is that things from that origin (or social class) have or lack virtue because of status. Therefore, the actual details of the argument can be overlooked.

PSYCHOGENETIC FALLACY: If you understand the psychological/political reason why your opponent likes an argument, therefore he's biased, thus his argument must be wrong by default.

ARGUMENT OF THE BEARD: Assuming that two ends of a spectrum are the same, since one can travel along the spectrum in small steps. The name comes from the idea that being clean-shaven must be the same as having a big beard.

ARGUMENT FROM AGE [WISDOM OF THE ANCIENTS]: Propagandizing the "fact" that an argument is superior due to age, appealing either through seniority (experience) or innovation (youth). Products marketed "New & Improved" appeal such a belief (i.e. innovation = value/strength).

NOT INVENTED HERE: Ideas from elsewhere are made unwelcome. This pertains to feelings that local ways/local identity are superior, and that innovations will only upset the established working system. Conversely, foreign or "imported" things may be held as superior.

ARGUMENT BY DISMISSAL: An idea is rejected without saying why.

ARGUMENT TO THE FUTURE: Arguing that evidence will someday be discovered which will then support your point.

POISONING THE WELLS: Discrediting the sources used by your opponents.

ARGUMENT BY EMOTIVE LANGUAGE [APPEAL TO THE PEOPLE]: Using emotionally loaded words to sway the audience's sentiments instead of their minds. Many emotions can be useful – anger, spite, envy, condescension, etc. "Guilty By Association" falls in this category.

ARGUMENT BY PERSONAL CHARM: Getting the audience to cut you slack. It helps greatly if you have a "flat" opponent. Charm may create trust or the desire to "join the winning team." This is intensified through "sex appeal."

APPEAL TO PITY/SYMPATHY: Self explanatory.

APPEAL TO FORCE: Threats, lawsuits, or even physical violence. The traditional religious threat is that one will burn in Hell.

BEGGING THE QUESTION [ASSUMING THE ANSWER]: "Circular Reasoning." The thing to be proved is used as one of your assumptions.

STOLEN CONCEPT: Utilizing what you are trying to disprove in order to disprove it. For example, using science to show that science is wrong.

ARGUMENT FROM AUTHORITY: The claim that the speaker is an expert, and therefore should be trusted. The speaker is actually claiming to be more expert in the subject area than anyone else in the room. There is also an implied claim that expertise in the area is worth having. For example, claiming expertise in something hopelessly quack.

ARGUMENT FROM FALSE AUTHORITY: "I'm not a Doctor, but I play one on TV."

APPEAL TO ANONYMOUS AUTHORITY: An appeal to authority is made, but the authority is not named. For example, "Experts agree," "scientists say," or the mysterious "they conclude." This makes the info impossible to verify.

APPEAL TO AUTHORITY: "Robert J. Oppenheimer was highly impressed by this theory." Yet a statement made by someone long-deceased could be out of date, or warped from a specific context.

APPEAL TO FALSE AUTHORITY: Using the statements of an authority to justify something outside their area of expertise. Another variation is to misquote a real authority out of context.

STATEMENT OF CONVERSION: "I used to believe in X." This is simply a weak form of asserting expertise. The speaker is implying that he has learned about the subject, and now that he is better informed, he has rejected X. Another variation: "I used to think that way when I was your age."

BAD ANALOGY: Claiming that two situations are highly similar, when they are not remotely so.

EXTENDED APOLOGY: The claim that two things, both analogous to a third thing, are therefore analogous to each other. The implication is that the position is somehow tainted through "guilt by association."

ARGUMENT FROM SPURIOUS SIMILARITY: It is suggested that any resemblance is factual proof of a direct relationship.

REIFYING: An abstract thing is talked about as if it were concrete.

FALSE CAUSE: Assuming that because two things happened, the first one caused the second.

CASUAL REDUCTIONISM [COMPLEX CAUSE]: Trying to use one cause to explain something, when in fact it had several causes.

CLICHÉ THINKING: Using as evidence a well-known "wise saying," as if it is directly proven.

EXCEPTION THAT PROVES THE RULE: This is used when a rule has been asserted, and someone points out the rule doesn't always work.

APPEAL TO WIDESPREAD BELIEF [BANDWAGON/PEER PRESSURE]: The claim that many people believe an idea, used to believe an idea, or currently enact it – therefore proving it's legitimacy.

FALLACY OF COMPOSITION: Assuming that a whole has the same simplicity as its constituent parts.

FALLACY OF DIVISION: Assuming that what is true of the whole is true of each constituent part.

COMPLEX QUESTION [TYING]: Unrelated points are treated as if they should be accepted or rejected together, when in reality each point should be accepted or rejected on its own merits.

SLIPPERY SLOPE FALLACY [CAMEL'S NOSE]: The assumption that something is wrong because it is right next to something that is wrong. Or it is wrong because it could slide towards something unwanted.

ARGUMENT BY PIGHEADEDNESS: Refusing to accept something after everyone else assumed it is proven fact.

APPEAL TO COINCIDENCE: Asserting that some fact is due to chance.

ARGUMENT BY REPETITION [ARGUMENT AD NAUSEAM]: If you say something often enough, some people will begin to believe it.

ARGUMENT BY HALF TRUTH [SUPPRESSED EVIDENCE]: Obvious.

ARGUMENT BY SELECTIVE OBSERVATION: "Cherry Picking."

ARGUMENT BY SELECTIVE READING: Making it seem as if the weakest of an opponent's arguments were the best he had.

ARGUMENT BY GENERALIZATION: Drawing a broad conclusion from a small number of unrepresentative cases.

MISUNDERSTANDING THE NATURE OF STATISTICS: Misinformation of statistical data.

NON SEQUITUR: Follow one concept with something that just does not follow the subject whatsoever.

MEANINGLESS QUESTIONS: Irresistible forces meeting immovable objects.

ARGUMENT BY POETIC LANGUAGE: If it sounds good, it must be right.

ARGUMENT BY SLOGAN: Being short, a slogan increases the effectiveness of "Argument By Repetition."

ARGUMENT BY PRESTIGIOUS JARGON: Using big complicated words so that you will seem to be an expert.

ARGUMENT BY GIBBERISH [BAFFLEMENT]: This is an extreme version of "ARGUMENT BY PRESTIGIOUS JARGON." Gibberish works effortlessly on people that can't find meaning in technical/prestigious jargon.

ARGUMENT BY POETIC LANGUAGE: Flowery = Confusion.

EQUIVOCATION: Using a word to mean one thing, and then later using it to mean something different.

EUPHEMISM: The use of words to cushion emotional response. The soldier was "sacrificed" in duty. The death of bystanders is "collateral damage."

WEASEL WORDING: This is very much like "EUPHEMISM," except that the word changes are done to claim a new, different concept rather than soften the old concept. For example, an American President may not conduct a war without a declaration of Congress. Therefore Military Operations are labeled "police actions", "armed incursions," "safeguarding American interests."

LIES: Intentional errors of fact.

HYPOTHESIS CONTRARY TO FACT: Arguing from something that might have happened, but did not.

INTERNAL CONTRADICTION: Saying two contradictory things in the same argument.

CHANGING THE SUBJECT [DIGRESSION/MISDIRECTION]: Easy Peazy.

ARGUMENT BY FAST TALKING: If you go from one idea to the next quickly enough, the audience won't have time to think.

AMBIGUOUS ASSERTION: A statement is made but it is unclear.

FAILURE TO STATE: If you make enough attacks, and ask enough questions, you may never have to actually define your own position.

OUTDATED INFORMATION: Information is given, but it is not the latest info on the subject.

LEAST PLAUSIBLE HYPOTHESIS: Ignoring all of the most reasonable explanations. This makes the desired explanation the only one.

ARGUMENT BY SCENARIO: Telling a story which ties together unrelated material, and then using the story as proof they are related.

MOVING THE GOALPOSTS: If your opponent successfully addresses some point, then say he must also address some further point. If you can make these points continually more difficult then eventually your opponent must fail.

APPEAL TO COMPLEXITY: If the Propagandist doesn't understand the topic, he concludes that nobody understands it.

COMMON SENSE: Each side thinks their answer is common sense. Clearly, some of these people are wrong. The reason they are wrong is because common sense depends on the context, knowledge & experience of the observer.

DISPROOF BY FALLACY: If a conclusion can be reached in an obviously fallacious way, then the conclusion is incorrectly declared wrong.

REDUCTIO AD ABSURDUM: Showing that your opponent's argument leads to some absurd conclusion.

FALSE COMPROMISE: If one does not understand a debate, it must be "fair" to split the difference, and agree on a compromise between the opinions.

FALLACY OF THE CRUCIAL EXPERIMENT: Claiming that some idea has been proved/disproved by a pivotal discovery.

PROPAGANDA IN MOTION: REQUIEM II

ARTICLE III: PSYOP STRATEGEMS
(PROPAGANA TECHNIQUES; AN ENCYCLOPEDIA MINOREM)

EXHIBIT A: CHARACTERISTICS OF CONTENT
SELF-EVIDENT

NATURE OF ARGUMENTS USED: An argument is a reason, or a series of reasons, offered as to why the audience should behave, believe, or think in a certain manner. An argument is expressed or implied.

INFERRED INTENT OF THE ORIGINATOR: This technique refers to the effect the Propagandist wishes to achieve on the target audience. "Divisive" & "Unifying" Propaganda fall within this technique.

SELF-EVIDENT TECHNIQUE/APPEAL TO AUTHORITY: Appeals to authority cite prominent figures to support a position, idea or course of action.

ASSERTION: Assertions are positive statements presented as fact. They imply that what is stated is self-evident and needs no further proof. Assertions may or may not be true.

BANDWAGON/INEVITABLE   VICTORY: "BANDWAGON" and "INEVITABLE VICTORY" persuade the audience to take a course of action *"everyone else is taking."* This technique reinforces the natural desire to be on *"the winning side."* This technique is used to convince the audience that a program is an expression of an irresistible mass movement that it is in their best interest to join. "INEVITABLE VICTORY" invites those not already on the bandwagon to join those currently aligned. Those partially on the bandwagon are reassured that staying aboard is the best course of action.

OBTAIN DISAPPROVAL: This technique is used to get the audience to disapprove of an action/idea by suggesting the idea is popular with groups that are hated/feared by the target audience.

GLITTERING GENERALITIES: Glittering generalities are emotionally charged words closely associated with valued concepts/beliefs that carry conviction without supporting information. They appeal to such emotions as love of country, home, peace, freedom, glory, honor, etc.

VAGUENESS: Generalities are deliberately vague so that the audience may supply their own interpretations. The intention is to move the audience by use of undefined phrases, without analyzing their validity or attempting to determine their reasonableness or application.

RATIONALIZATION: Individuals or groups may use favorable generalities to rationalize questionable acts or beliefs. Vague and pleasant phrases are often used to justify such actions or beliefs.

SIMPLIFICATION: Favorable generalities are used to provide simple answers to complex social, political, economic, or military problems.

TRANSFER: This is a technique of projecting positive or negative qualities (*praise/blame*) of a person, entity, object, or value (*an individual, group, organization, nation, patriotism, etc*) to another in order to make the second more acceptable or to discredit it. This technique is generally used to transfer blame from one member of a conflict to another.

LEAST OF EVILS: Acknowledging that the course of action being taken is perhaps undesirable but that any alternative would result in an outcome far worse. This technique is used to explain the need for sacrifices or to justify things which displease the target audience or restrict their personal liberties.

NAME CALLING: This technique attempts to arouse prejudices in an audience by labeling the object of the Propaganda campaign as something the target audience fears, hates, loathes, or finds undesirable.

PINPOINTING THE OPPOSITION: A complex situation is reduced to a simplified "*enemy*" which as the source of all woes.

PLAIN FOLKS: The "*Plain Folks*" approach attempts to convince the audience that positions reflect the common sense of the people. It is designed to win the confidence of the audience by communicating in the common manner/speech/style of the direct audience.

Presenting soldiers as Plain Folks: The Propagandist wants to make the enemy feel he is fighting against soldiers who are "*decent, everyday folks;*" this helps to counter themes that paint the opponent as a "*bloodthirsty killer.*"

Presenting civilians as Plain Folks: The "Plain Folks" device also can help to convince the enemy that the opposing nation is not composed of arrogant, immoral, deceitful, aggressive, warmongering people – but rather of people wishing to live at peace.

Humanizing leaders: Paints a more human portrait of aligned military/civilian leaders. It humanizes them so that the audience looks upon them as similar human beings or as kind, wise, fatherly figures.

Vernacular: This is the contemporary language of a specific region or people as it is commonly spoken/written and includes songs/idioms/jokes. The current vernacular of the specific target audience must be utilized.

Dialect: Dialect is a variation in pronunciation/grammar/vocabulary from the norm of a region/nation.

Errors: To give the impression of spontaneity, deliberately hesitate between phrases, stammer, or mispronounce words.

HOMEY WORDS: Homey words are forms of "*virtue words*" – "*home,*" "*family,*" "*children,*" "*farm,*" "*neighbors.*" They evoke a favorable emotional response and help transfer the sympathies of the audience to the Propagandist. Homey words are widely used to evoke nostalgia.

SOCIAL DISAPPROVAL: This is a technique by which the Propagandist suggests that attitudes/actions contrary to the one outlined will only result in social rejection, disapproval, or ostracism.

VIRTUE WORDS: These are words in the value system of the target audience which tend to produce a positive image when attached to a person/issue. *"Peace," "happiness," "security," "wise leadership," "freedom."*

SLOGANS: A slogan is a brief, striking phrase that may include labeling/stereotyping. Effective slogans are self-perpetuating.

TESTIMONIALS: Testimonials are quotations, in or out of context – especially cited to support or reject a given policy, action, program, or personality. The reputation or role (*expert / authority*) of the individual giving the statement is exploited. The testimonial places the official sanction of a respected authority onto a Propagandic message. This is done in an effort to cause the target audience to identify itself with the authority or to accept the authority's opinions and beliefs as its own.

types of testimonials

I. Official Sanction: The testimonial authority must have given the endorsement or be clearly on record as having approved the attributed idea, concept, action, or belief. Four factors are involved –– *Accomplishment, Identification With The Target, Position of Authority, Inanimate Objects.*

*Accomplishment. People have confidence in an authority who has demonstrated outstanding ability and proficiency in his field.

Identification with the target. People have greater confidence in an authority with whom they have a common bond. For example, the soldier more readily trusts an officer with whom he has undergone likewise experiences..

Position of authority. The official position of authority may instill confidence.

Inanimate objects. Inanimate objects may be used in the testimonial device. Mount Rushmore, for example, conveys patriotism.

II. Personal Sources/Testimonial Authority: There are four major archetypes that fall into this category, best demonstrated in military terms – *Enemy Leaders, Fellow Soldiers, Opposing Leaders & Noteworthy Academia*.

Enemy leaders. The enemy target audience will generally place great value on its high level military leaders as a source of information.

Fellow soldiers. Those in the military are more inclined to accept what other soldiers have to say.

Opposing leaders. Testimonials of leaders of the opposing nation are of particular value in messages that outline war aims and objectives for administering the enemy nation after it capitulates.

Noteworthy Academia. Famous scholars, writers, and other personalities.

III. Nonpersonal Sources of Testimonial Authority: Institutions, ideologies, national flags, religious, and other non-personal sources are often used. The creeds, beliefs, principles, or dogmas of respected authorities or other public figures may make effective testimonials.

EXHIBIT B: CHARACTERISTICS OF THE CONTENT REQUIRING ADDITIONAL INFORMATION TO BE RECOGNIZED

INSINUATION: Insinuation is used to create or stir up the suspicions against ideas, groups, or individuals in order to divide an opposition camp.

I) Ideological differences between the opposition and its allies/satellites. II) Cultural/ethnic/territorial differences. III) Religious/economic/political differences. IV) History of civilian animosity/unfair treatment towards opposition supporters. V) People versus the bureaucracy/hierarchy. VII) Political differences between the ruling elite and their associates VIII) Differences illuminating an economic minority that is benefiting at the expense of the majority. IX) Unequal or inequitable tax burdens, or the high level of taxes; hidden taxes. X) The scarcity of consumer goods for the general public and their availability to the various elites and the dishonest. XI) Costs of present government policies in terms of lost opportunities to accomplish constructive socially desirable goals. XII) The powerlessness of the individual.

"insinuation devices" available to exploit similar vulnerabilities

LEADING QUESTIONS: The Propagandist may ask questions which suggest only one possible answer.

HUMOR: Humor can be an effective form of insinuation. Jokes and cartoons about the enemy find a ready audience among those persons in the target country or military camp who normally reject straightforward accusations.

PURE MOTIVES: Acting in the best interests of the target audience, insinuating that the enemy is acting to the contrary.

GUILT BY ASSOCIATION: Guilt by association links a person, group, or idea to other persons, groups, or ideas repugnant to the target audience.

RUMOR: Malicious rumors are highly effective.

PICTORIAL/PHOTOGRAPHIC PROPAGANDA: A photo, picture, or cartoon can insinuate a derogatory charge more effectively than words.

CARD STACKING/SELECTIVE OMISSION: This is the process of choosing from a variety of facts only those which support the Propagandist's purpose. Facts are selected and presented which most effectively strengthen and authenticate the point of view of the Propagandist. Card stacking, case making, and censorship are all forms of selection.

INCREASE PRESTIGE: Publicizing the best qualities of the institutions, concepts, or persons.

SIMPLIFICATION: Many facts of a situation are reduced so that the right / wrong of an action / decision is "obvious." This provides simple solutions.

– simplification maintains following characteristics –

IT THINKS FOR OTHERS: Some people accept information which they cannot verify personally as long as the source or the authority is considered expert. Others absorb info with little discrimination.

IT IS CONCISE: Simplification gives the impression of going to the heart of the matter in a few words. The target audience will not even consider that there may be another answer.

EXHIBIT C: CHARACTERISTICS OF CONTENT MAY BECOME EVIDENT WHEN NUMEROUS PIECES OF OUTPUT ARE EXAMINED

CHANGE OF PACE: Change of pace is a technique of switching from belligerent to peaceful output, from "hot" to "cold," from persuasion to threat, from emotion to fact.

STALLING: Stalling is a technique of deliberately withholding information.

SHIFT OF SCENE: Attempting to take the spotlight off an unfavorable situation/condition by shifting it to another.

REPETITION: An idea is repeated in an attempt to elicit an almost automatic response or to reinforce an audience's opinion or attitude.

FEAR OF CHANGE: People fear change – particularly sudden, imposed change over which they have no control. That is why every successful psychological campaign must give offer a reasonably safe, honorable way out of any difficult predicament or situation.

::: Zeero Xiron // 4.4.2025 :::

Zeero Xiron emerged from The Void – a total renegade from Parts Unknown. Under another

Alias, he puts out books & music as some other guy.

Zeero Xiron is a Magickal Supervillain + aspiring Heretic Ipsissimus practicing Cosmic Witchcraft & High Magick upon a framework of Heretic Druidry, Qabalah, Ninjutsu, Hermetic & Pythagorean Philosophy.

Z.X. promotes Spiritual & Psychological Alchemy, Ritual Magick, Tarot & more. Xiron is a non-Abrahamic Monotheist who observes Architect & Creation.

Regardless, this weird freak is a Pagan in that they worship nature in a universal sense + accept many Deities & Daemons as valid masks & aspects of The Creation.

Zeero Xiron is a mysterious Social Media personality offering Sweets to the Sweet for the Finest Freaks. Z.X. can be found via Dr. Zeero Xiron Free Magick Secrets Show on Youtube, TikTok, Instagram, Patreon.

Welcome to the Wonder-filled World of Zeero Xiron
** Contact // ZeeroXiron@GMX.com **

This is the First Book by Neron Press

Made in United States
Troutdale, OR
05/21/2025

31541345R00100